sources from the ancient near east

volume 2, fascicle 1

reconstructing history from

ancient inscriptions:

the lagash-umma border conflict

revised third printing

by

jerrold s. cooper

undena publications

malibu 1983

A Publication of
IIMAS
International Institute for Mesopotamian Area Studies

SOURCES AND MONOGRAPHS ON THE ANCIENT NEAR EAST

Editors: Giorgio Buccellati, Marilyn Kelly-Buccellati
Assistant Editor: Patricia Oliansky

These two series make available original documents in English translation (Sources) and important studies by modern scholars (Monographs) as a contribution to the study of the history, religion, literature, art, and archaeology of the Ancient Near East. Inexpensive and flexible in format, they are meant to serve the specialist by bringing within easy reach basic publications, often in updated versions, to provide imaginative education outlets for undergraduate and graduate courses, and to reach interested segments of the educated lay audience.

SANE 2/1

Reconstructing History from Ancient Inscriptions:
The Lagash-Umma Border Conflict by *J. S. Cooper*

The Lagash-Umma border dispute is the earliest well-documented interstate conflict known. From about 2500 to 2350 B.C., the Sumerian city-states of Lagash and Umma contested the right to exploit a tract of land on their common border, and their dispute is documented by a series of inscriptions filled with claims and counterclaims, and sometimes vivid descriptions of battles between the two states.

This volume makes available for the first time, complete English translations of all documents relevant to these events. After a brief introduction to early civilization and political organization in Babylonia, the documents are described in detail. There follows an exposition of the difficulties involved in trying to reconstruct the chronology and the geography of the conflict, and the philological problems that hamper our understanding of the documents. The actual reconstruction of the 150 year struggle is then undertaken, by critically examining the sources for each episode. An attempt is made to account for both the high degree of agreement among the individual sources, and the occasional glaring discrepancies.

Documents from outside the corpus of texts relating the border conflict, and archeological evidence, are used to set the Lagash-Umma dispute in the broader context of third millennium Mesopotamian history. Special attention is paid to the art and language of ancient historical narratives and the limits they place on the nature of the historical data that can be elicited from a close reading of the inscriptions. The volume is intended both for specialists and for teachers and students of ancient history in general.

Grateful acknowledgment is made for permission to reproduce maps
from *RGTC* 1 to the *Tübinger Atlas des vorderen Orients* and the L. Reichert Verlag, Wiesbaden.

ISBN: 0-89003-059-6

For JOB

" . . . the men in France play a very active part
in everything that pertains to the kitchen."
Alice B. Toklas

What is involved, then, in that finding of the "true story," that discovery of the "real story" within or behind the events that come to us in the chaotic form of "historical records"? What wish is enacted, what desire is gratified, by the fantasy that *real* events are properly represented when they can be shown to display the formal coherency of a story?

Hayden White, in W.J.T. Mitchell (ed.),
On Narrative

CONTENTS

Preface to the Third Edition 3

Preface 5

Abbreviations 6

Note on Transcription 6

Note on References 6

Chapter I   Introduction: Early Civilization and Political Organization in Babylonia 7

Chapter II   Sources for the Reconstruction of the Lagash-Umma Conflict 12

Chapter III   Difficulties in Reconstruction 18
    1. Geographical problems 18
    2. Chronological problems 19
    3. Philological problems 20

Chapter IV   The Border Conflict Reconstructed 22
    1. Before Urnanshe 22
    2. Urnanshe and Akurgal 23
    3. Eanatum 24
    4. Enanatum I 28
    5. Enmetena 30
    6. Uru'inimgina 33
    7. Conclusion 36

Chapter V   Historical Tradition and the Language of History 38

Chapter VI   The Documents in Translation 44
    1. Urnanshe 44
    2. Eanatum (Stela of the Vultures) 45
    3. Eanatum (Boulders) 48
    4. Eanatum (Clay Vase) 48
    5. Enanatum I 49
    6. Enmetena 49
    7. Uru'inimgina (Clay Dish) 51
    8. Uru'inimgina (Cylinder Fragment) 52
    9. Uru'inimgina (Clay Tablet) 52
  10. Lugalzagesi 52
  11. Ruler's name not preserved (Clay Vessel Fragment) 53
  12. Ruler's name not preserved (Clay Vessel Fragment) 53

Maps 57

Charts 60

Plates . . . . after p. 28

MAPS

1. Mesopotamia and its Neighbors in the Presargonic and Sargonic Periods 57
    (from *RGTC* 1)
2. Babylonia and Western Iran in the Presargonic and Sargonic Periods 58
    (from *RGTC* 1)
3. Sumer in the Presargonic Period 59
    (from Jacobsen, *Sumer* 25, p. 109)

CHARTS

1. Rulers of the Presargonic Period 60
2. Important Gods Mentioned in the Documents of Chapter VI 61

ILLUSTRATIONS

1. Eanatum Leading his Troops (Stela of the Vultures) I
2. A Burial Mound of Fallen Ummaites (Stela of the Vultures) II
3. Enmetena's "Cone" (Text No. 6) III
4. The "Frontier of Shara" (Text No. 10) IV

PREFACE TO THE THIRD PRINTING

Much progress has been made in the study of third millennium B.C. Mesopotamia in the twenty years since this booklet was first published. Nevertheless I believe the interpretations offered here remain sound.

Corrections in detail, improvements in translation, and recent bibliography will be found in D. Frayne's forthcoming volume, *Presargonic Period*, in the series Royal Inscriptions of Mesopotamia. Readers will also find a helpful guide in J. Bauer, R. Englund, and M. Krebernik, *Mesopotamien: Späturuk-Zeit und Frühdynastische Zeit* (Fribourg 1998).

I would, however, like to point out a few important changes wrought by time. The king of Kish, Al [   ] (Text No. 2; p. 26; Chart 1) has been shown by Irene Winter to be a phantom. The name of the last ruler of Lagash, read here Uru'inimgina, is once again being read Uru-kagina, or now, Irikagina. And Text No. 10, which defines the Lagash-Umma border according to Umma, is not to be attributed to Lugalzagesi, as had been thought, but to a slightly earlier ruler of Umma, Gishakidu. Consult Frayne for detail on all of these changes.

Finally, my thanks to Undena Publications for making it possible to correct a few minor typographical errors, and for keeping this study in print.

J.S.C.

PREFACE

While preparing the translations for the first volume of *Sumerian and Akkadian Royal Inscriptions* (*SARI*), it became clear that I could not possibly justify my understanding of the inscriptions dealing with the conflict between Lagash and Umma without setting forth my interpretation of the conflict itself. Since an historical essay of this sort would be inappropriate to the format of the series, I decided to prepare an independent study of the conflict, which could later be cited in the notes to the translations, when necessary. This decision made, I soon rejected the notion of writing a traditional monograph or long journal article on the subject. The inscriptions—many known since the beginning of the century—and the conflict itself have been the subject of numerous studies (see the bibliography). To systematically cite and refute or accept the interpretations of even only the most important of these at every relevant moment of my exposition would be a wearisome chore, and ensure a readership of only a narrow group of specialists.

Writing for the *SANE* series not only provides a certain flexibility that allows me to be interpretive without being pedantic, it also provides the opportunity to show students and non-specialists what Mesopotamian history is made of. By presenting the sources, in translation, and a discussion of their problems, the difficulties as well as the possibilities of writing the history of ancient Babylonia can be demonstrated. These particular texts are of special interest because they constitute an unusually rich dossier concerning a long-standing inter-state territorial conflict, which is the earliest well-documented conflict of this kind known.

In my reconstruction of the conflict I have tried to steer a middle course between a harmonized resumé of the contents of the inscriptions on the one hand, and an imaginative fleshing out of the inscriptions' bare bones on the other. There is no point to the former; the translations alone would do. But an excess of imagination, whether in the restoration of hopelessly broken passages, or in supplying all the information that the texts are presumed to have omitted, yields a reconstruction of events so much closer to the possible than the probable, that it cannot be seriously considered by the historian.

I am all too aware of the limits of both my method and my results, but I believe my reconstruction to be sober if tentative, and as far as we can go at this time without much more basic research and analysis of the written and archeological remains of the late Early Dynastic period.

Work on this study was generously supported by the National Endowment for the Humanities. I am grateful to it and to the Johns Hopkins University for the leisure to study, contemplate and write. I would also like to thank colleagues and friends in Paris and Berkeley whose hospitality greatly enhanced the conditions under which this study was produced. The many useful suggestions made by colleagues regarding specific translations and interpretations will be more completely acknowledged in *SARI*, but mention must be made here of the generosity of Horst Steible and Hermann Behrens, who provided me with a manuscript of their just published *Die altsumerische Bau- und Weihinschriften*. Special thanks go to Pat Oliansky for her careful editorial attention and guidance.

ABBREVIATIONS

ABW	Altsumerische Bau- und Weihinschriften (Bibl. IV)
CAH	Cambridge Ancient History (Bibl. IA)
ED	Early Dynastic
IRSA	Inscriptions royales sumériennes et akkadiennes (Bibl. IV)
RGTC	Répertoire géographique des textes cunéiformes (Bibl. IB)
RLA	Reallexikon der Assyriologie (Bibl. IA)
SARI	Sumerian and Akkadian Royal Inscriptions (Bibl. IV)
UET	Ur Excavations. Texts

NOTE ON TRANSCRIPTION

Sumerian words and names have been transcribed without diacritics.

The letter /h/ is always /ḫ/, pronounced like /ch/ in German *ach*;

Sumerian /g̃/ (ng) has not been distinguished from /g/. The actual reading of many Sumerian words and names is uncertain, but the scholarly practice of capitalizing those parts of words and names that are uncertain has not been maintained here.

NOTE ON REFERENCES

Three kinds of references are given in parentheses in the body of the text. Roman numerals alone or followed by an Arabic numeral (e.g. V, IV.6) refer the reader to chapters or sections of chapters. Arabic numerals preceded by "No." (e.g. No. 6) refer to the numbered translated inscriptions in Chapter VI. References to works in the Bibliography are preceded by "Bibl.," followed by the section of the Bibliography in which they can be found.

CHAPTER I

Introduction: Early Civilization and Political Organization in Babylonia[1]

The earliest large urban agglomoration in Mesopotamia was the city known as Uruk in later texts. There, around 3000 B.C., certain distinctive features of historic Mesopotamian civilization emerged: the cylinder seal, a system of writing that soon became cuneiform, a repertoire of religious symbolism, and various artistic and architectural motifs and conventions.[2] Another feature of Mesopotamian civilization in the early historic periods, the constellation of more or less independent city-states resistant to the establishment of a strong central political force, was probably characteristic of this proto-historic period as well. Uruk, by virtue of its size, must have played a dominant role in southern Babylonia, and the city of Kish probably played a similar role in the north.

From the period that archaeologists call Early Dynastic II (ED II), beginning about 2700 B.C.,[3] the appearance of walls around Babylonian cities suggests that inter-city warfare had become institutionalized. The earliest royal inscriptions, which date to this period, belong to kings of Kish, a northern Babylonian city, but were found in the Diyala region, at Nippur, at Adab and at Girsu. Those at Adab and Girsu are from the later part of ED II and are in the name of Mesalim, king of Kish, accompanied by the names of the respective local rulers.[4] The king of Kish thus exercised hegemony far beyond the walls of his own city, and the memory of this particular king survived in native historical traditions for centuries: the Lagash-Umma border was represented in the inscriptions from Lagash as having been determined by the god Enlil, but actually drawn by Mesalim, king of Kish (IV.1). As a result of this early hegemony, the title "king of Kish" came to be used as a prestige title by any Babylonian ruler strong enough to exercise some sort of hegemony over all of Babylonia, or at least over the northern part.[5]

By the beginning of Early Dynastic III (ED III), around 2500 B.C., this northern part

---

[1] See section I A of the bibliography for the basic introductions to ancient Mesopotamia in general and the late Presargonic period in particular. It will be assumed that the nonspecialist reader has acquainted himself with at least the works of Oppenheim, Kramer and Bottéro listed there.

A somewhat different account of the political organization of late Presargonic Sumer can be found in Westenholz (Bibl. III). The theory of a Sumerian league with one "great king" is, for me stretching the evidence (though new evidence may make it more probable). For Jacobsen's evidence for such a league in the Fara tablets (Bibl. III), see the reservations expressed by Edzard in *Orientalia Lovaniensia Analecta* 5-6, 153ff.

[2] On Uruk, see Adams and Nissen, *The Uruk Countryside*. For cylinder seals, see the recent Introduction in Porada, *Ancient Art in Seals*. For the archaic tablets from Uruk, see Green, *Journal of Near Eastern Studies* 39, 1ff., with bibliography and an excellent example of what can and cannot be retrieved from a careful study of these texts.

[3] For the Early Dynastic sequence, see Porada in Ehrich (Bibl. IC). The absolute dates are very approximate, and may have to be moved up or back by as much as a century. The Early Dynastic period, especially the later part, is also known as Presargonic, i.e. before Sargon of Agade brought all of Mesopotamia under his control, around 2300 B.C.

[4] *SARI* Ki 3, *IRSA* I A 3, *ABW* Mes. v. Kiš 1f.

[5] Edzard, *RLA* 5,608 suggests that an empire of Kish never existed; Kish was simply the name for northern Babylonia, as Akkad was to become after Sargon. But given the example of Akkad itself (from Sargon's

of Babylonia, that is, the part north of Nippur, must have had a rather important population of speakers of the Semitic language known in its later phases as Akkadian.[6] The first Semitic personal names in Babylonia are attested from about 2500 B.C. at Kish and at Abu Salabikh near Nippur, approximately contemporary with (or somewhat earlier than) the Ebla texts from northern Syria, which provide evidence for a Semitic language different than, but closely related to, Old Akkadian.[7] Our sources for the history of ED III do not allow us to say much about the role, if any, of this ethno-linguistic heterogeneity (Semites of various persuasions, Sumerians, and, no doubt, others) in inter-state conflicts. The extant Mesopotamian sources are in Sumerian, and never refer to the ethno-linguistic affiliations of either allies or enemies.[8]

These sources, primarily royal inscriptions, tell us all too little about the political history of the period.[9] The great exception is the corpus of inscriptions of the rulers of Lagash, for the most part excavated by the French at Tello (ancient Girsu) beginning a century ago, and augmented in recent years by some important finds of the American expedition to Al-Hiba (ancient Lagash). The state of Lagash itself consisted of three major cities, Girsu (Tello), Lagash (Al-Hiba), and Nina (Surghul), as well as many smaller settlements.[10] So, too, the neighbor and antagonist of Lagash, the state of Umma, must be considered not just as the city Umma itself, but as a broader territory including at least one other major city, Zabala (IV.5). We know nothing about the origin of the union of the three cities comprising the state of Lagash; the texts take it for granted, and it goes back at least to the time of Mesalim (ED II). Curiously, the state itself is called Lagash, the name of one of these three cities, but the chief deity of the state is Ningirsu, whose name means "Lord of Girsu." A later union of two cities, in ED III, is that of Uruk and Ur. The first ruler to effect that union, a contemporary of Enmetena of Lagash, tells us explicitly in his inscriptions that he did so (V), and this union of Uruk and Ur eventually included Umma as well (IV.6). But already in the time of Urnanshe, three generations earlier, there is evidence for joint operations

---

capital Agade), and of Babylonia and Assyria in later periods (from the cities Babylon and Assur respectively), it is unthinkable that the city Kish would give its name to northern Babylonia if it had not at one time dominated that area. See now Gelb, "Ebla and the Kish Civilization" (Bibl. III).

[6] See the recent remarks of Westenholz (Bibl. III) on Semitic and Sumerian in early Babylonia, and see now Gelb's speculations on Kishite Semitic (Bibl. III, 69ff.).

[7] Pettinato (Bibl. III) chap. IV; Gelb, "Thoughts About Ibla," *Syro-Mesopotamian Studies* 1/1. Gelb now dates the Kish personal names slightly earlier than Fara, the Abu Salabikh texts slightly later than Fara, and Ebla somewhat later than Abu Salabikh. He also suggests that the administrative texts from Abu Salabikh are written in logographic Semitic (Bibl. III, 55ff.).

[8] There are a few inscriptions from Mesopotamia proper that, by virtue of a Semitic pronoun, betray the fact that they were read in Semitic, although written in Sumerian (most such inscriptions are from Mari). Another group of inscriptions, while having no Semitic elements at all, is written in a style that some scholars believe indicates that they were read in Semitic. See now Gelb (Bibl. III).

Westenholz (Bibl. III) has advanced the hypothesis that ethnolinguistic differences *were* important in the political history of ED III (Bibl. III). For the opposing view, see Cooper, *Orientalia* 42, 239ff. and Jacobsen, *Archiv fuer Orientforschung* 26, 8ff.

[9] This has more to do with circumstances of preservation and discovery than with any "sumerische Thematik" (Kienast, *Oriens Antiquus* 19, 247ff.). Building inscriptions are both more likely to be duplicated (bricks and clay nails) and to survive (especially foundation deposits). Historical inscriptions, however, are often on stelas, whose stone is likely to be reused or looted, or on a variety of unusual objects which would not have been produced in large numbers, or whose placement may have been either very exposed (e.g. the copper standard of No. 5) or very remote (pots and cones inscribed with the texts of Nos. 6 and 10 may have been implanted on or near the Lagash-Umma border).

[10] See Falkenstein (Bibl. IB), 17ff.

against Lagash by Ur to the southwest, and Umma to the northwest. In Sumer, then, our sources lend themselves to the following reconstruction of the geo-political environment in ED III: Political power was concentrated in the city-states of Ur and Uruk to the southwest, Umma (-Zabala) to the north, and Lagash (-Girsu-Nina) in the east. For Lagash, battling the states to the southwest and northwest, often acting in concert, was a major preoccupation. The union of Uruk and Ur, with its eventual absorption of Umma, had the effect (if not the purpose) of isolating Lagash in Sumer.[11] In northern Babylonia, a possible union between the cities of Kish and Akshak is suggested by the alliance between them attested in inscriptions of both Eanatum (IV.3) and, three or more generations later, Enshakushana.[12]

Interstate conflicts attested in the inscriptions of ED III are of two types: those with neighboring city-states, like the Lagash-Umma conflict, had to do with land and water rights;[13] those with more distant states either were related to more local conflicts—for example, Urluma's use of foreign troops in the texts treated below—or in all probability involved attempts to loot supplies of raw materials (raids from Babylonia to outlying areas) or finished goods (raids on Babylonian cities). The documents discussed in this study illustrate the first type. The second is well-illustrated by a letter of Lu'ena, a temple administrator on the southeastern edge of the territory of Lagash, to Enentarzi, then temple administrator at Girsu during the reign of Enanatum II. Lu'ena reports that he intercepted a force of "600 Elamites from Lagash who were carrying booty to Elam."[14] But, of course, looting was not limited only to long-distance raids, as is clear from our text No. 9.

The rulers in whose name these inscriptions are written call themselves and each other by a variety of titles, and despite several studies devoted to this subject, their precise nuances remain unclear.[15] The least specific title is *lú*, literally "man," which I translate "leader."[16] It is most frequently used when talking about rulers of other states without giving their personal names. Text No. 6, for example, talks of "the 'leader' (*lú*) of Umma," but "Urluma, 'ruler' (*ensí*) of Umma." The word translated "ruler," Sumerian *ensí*, is the title taken most frequently by the rulers of Lagash. Its etymology is uncertain, and in the following periods of Mesopotamian history (Sargonic and Third Dynasty of Ur) it is used as the title of provincial governors.[17] But in ED III, it is primarily a title taken by the

[11] This early isolation could explain in part the complete omission of Lagash in the Sumerian King List, a traditional account of early dynasties and rulers of Babylonia (Kramer, Bibl. IA, 328ff.; cf. Edzard, *RLA* 6, 77ff., and note the [satirical?] Lagash Kinglist published by Sollberger, *Journal of Cuneiform Studies* 21,279ff.). But why then, were e.g. Kish, Anshan and Mari included?

[12] *SARI* Uk 4.1, *IRSA* IH1b, *ABW* Enš. v. Uruk 1 and 3.

[13] Nissen (Bibl. III) sees the vulnerability of downstream cities' water supplies to diversion by upstream neighbors as a major source of inter-city conflict in ED III.

[14] Grégoire (Bibl. III) 9ff.

[15] See Edzard's discussion in *RLA* 4,335ff.

[16] For a similar use of Akkadian *awēlum* "man," see *Chicago Assyrian Dictionary* A/2,57.

[17] Whether *ensí* also denotes a subordinate in ED III is a subject of controversy. The inscriptions of Mesalim, just before the beginning of this period, name him as "king of Kish" and address the local rulers as *ensí*, but most see this as an overlord-local independent ruler relationship, not one of king and governor. But at the end of ED III, there is evidence both in Lagash (Bauer, *Welt des Orients* 9,1f.) and Umma (Powell, Bibl. III, 27) that there were *ensí*s directly subordinate to *lugal*s, much as they would be in the following periods. Powell denies that the evidence demonstrates this (Bibl. III, 27ff.), but a copy of the caption on a monument of Sargon celebrating the defeat of Lugalzagesi, who began his career as ruler of Umma, then became king of Uruk and extended his domination over all of Sumer (IV.6), does prove that while Lugalzagesi was king of Uruk, there was a separate individual subordinate to him who bore the title *ensí* of Umma. The caption reads "Lugalzagesi, king (*lugal*) of Uruk; Mese, *ensí* of Umma," then breaks off (*Archiv fuer Orientforschung* 20,37).

independent rulers at Lagash (as well as by some rulers of other cities), and used by the rulers of Lagash to describe foreign rulers who, in their own inscriptions, call themselves "king." The title traditionally translated "king," and which is taken by nearly all independent rulers in the following periods, is Sumerian *lugal*, literally "big man." Relatively rare at Lagash, it is the most common title used by independent rulers of other cities in ED III.[18]

We know very little about how rulers exercised power in this period. Their inscriptions, quite naturally, picture them wielding power absolutely, with the help and support of the gods. Administrative documents from Girsu inform us of a wealth of officials, but rarely have to do with political matters. Documents from Zabala that record land grants made by Lugalzagesi to officials of Adab and Nippur reveal something of the economic basis of the ruler's power, and the non-military side of empire building.[19] The letter of Lu'ena cited above points to the importance of the *sanga* or temple-estate administrator. Since much of the economy of Lagash (and other cities) was controlled by the ruler through large land-holding organizations centered around the temples of major deities, the administrators of these organizations were powerful individuals.[20] When Urluma of Umma was killed after being defeated by Enanatum I of Lagash, he was succeeded as ruler by his nephew Il, who was *sanga* at Zabala (IV.5). Similarly, Enentarzi was first *sanga* at Girsu before he became ruler of Lagash.[21] Although nominally controlled by the ruler, the temple organizations must have been influential centers of power in their own right, and the famous Reform Texts of Uru'inimgina, of which No. 7 is an example, demonstrate an unmistakable, if poorly understood, conflict of interest between the *sanga*s and their organizations, and the royal family.[22]

Evidence for inter-state relations is scanty. The alliances and coalitions that appear in the inscriptions suggest that something like the elaborate system of ambassadors and diplomatic missions documented for the Old Babylonian period 500 years later was already operative in the Presargonic period. Several of the texts discussed below mention messages sent between Lagash and Umma, and even pretend to quote them verbatim (V). There is no reason to think this communication between states was in any way exceptional. A famous inscription of Enmetena tells us that "Enmetena, ruler of Lagash, and Lugalkiginedudu, ruler of Uruk, established brotherhood (between themselves)." Traditionally it has been assumed that this attested to a treaty or alliance between the two city-states, but new documents show that the relationship between them must have been rather complicated, and the exact meaning of the "brotherhood" text is uncertain (IV.5). But whatever that meaning may be, the inscription remains the earliest attestation for a formal interstate relationship in Babylonia. The recently excavated archives at Ebla in northern Syria confirm that such relationships were widespread, and certainly antedate our extant evidence.[23]

Trade must have played a large role in inter-state relations, both directly and indirectly.

---

[18] For the title *en*, associated with the city Uruk, and not occurring in our dossier, see Edzard, *RLA* 4, 336.

[19] See Charvát (Bibl. III); Powell (Bibl. III), 29.

[20] On the subject of land tenure and the role of temple organizations in Presargonic Lagash, see most recently Maekawa (Bibl. III) and Foster (Bibl. III). Similar conditions prevailed at Umma-Zabala according to Powell (Bibl. III), 25f.: "The ties between the head of state and the temple are very close, so close, in fact, that the lines dividing temple and state are not perceptible."

[21] See Grégoire (Bibl. III), 14 for the possible relationship of Enentarzi to the Urnanshe dynasty, of which Enanatum II (Enentarzi's predecessor) is the last certain member.

[22] Cf. Maekawa (Bibl. III).

[23] Pettinato (Bibl. III), 95ff.; Sollberger, *Studi Eblaiti* 3,129ff.; Edzard, *Studi Eblaiti* 4,89ff.

At Lagash, Urnanshe, the founder of the dynasty that dominates our study, claims repeatedly that "he had ships of Dilmun transport timber (to Lagash) from foreign lands."[24] The administrative documents from Girsu at the end of our period mention commercial exchanges with Adab, Der, Nippur, Umma and Uruk in Babylonia, and the more distant Dilmun, Elam, Mishime, Urua and Uruaz.[25] This trade was usually conducted by commercial agents (*damgar*) of the large institutions, and is sometimes represented as exchanges between royal families or with foreign rulers.[26] We have no information about trade agreements, nor is there any direct reference in the inscriptions to struggles for the control of trade routes. But their importance is attested to by the long inscription of Lugalzagesi found at Nippur, which states that after Enlil made Lugalzagesi king of all Sumer, "from the Lower Sea (Persian Gulf), (along) the Tigris and Euphrates to the Upper Sea (Mediterranean), he (Enlil) put their routes in good order for him."[27] Lagash, on Sumer's southeastern flank, must have been especially well-situated for the Persian Gulf trade and trade with Elam (southwestern Iran).

Theoretically, the Sumerican city was the property of the chief god of that city, and he took an active role in its affairs. What this meant in reality is not entirely clear, but the texts in our dossier picture boundaries decided by and between gods (IV.1), gods intervening on the battlefield and elsewhere (V), gods suckling future kings (No. 2 iv), and gods called upon to punish offenders (e.g. No. 9).[28] The theory of divine ownership explains why so much of a city's land and other economic resources were administered through temple organizations, as mentioned earlier. Most important among the gods for us is Ningirsu, chief of the pantheon of Lagash. The territory that is the subject of the Lagash-Umma border conflict, an area called the Gu'edena ("Edge of the Plain"), is his "beloved field," and it is to restore this territory to Ningirsu that Lagash battles Umma. This theological rationale of all Mesopotamian imperialism—making war in the name of a god for territory claimed by a god or given to the warring ruler by a god—was thus present at the beginning of recorded Babylonian history. It persisted in royal inscriptions through two millennia and figured prominently in the propaganda of Cyrus the Persian when he justified bringing the last independent Babylonian kingdom to an end.[29]

[24] E.g. *SARI* La 1.12-14.

[25] M. Lambert, *Revue d'Assyriologie* 47,57ff., *Archiv Orientalni* 23,566ff., *Oriens Antiquus* 20,175ff.

[26] *Revue d'Assyriologie* 57,58f., exchanges between Baranamtara, wife of Lugalanda of Lagash, and the wife of the ruler of Adab; *ibid.*, 64f., a shipment of grain and metal to the ruler of Urua.

[27] *SARI* Um 7.1 ii.

[28] See Maekawa (Bibl. III) and Foster (Bibl. III) for various theories of divine ownership as they apply to the socio-economic organization of the state.

[29] Oppenheim in Pritchard, *Ancient Near Eastern Texts* (3rd ed.), 315f.

CHAPTER II

Sources For The Reconstruction of The Lagash-Umma Conflict

The documents that provide the basis for our reconstruction are all written in the Sumerian language in cuneiform characters, on artifacts of stone or clay. Phrases are grouped in ruled rectangles called cases, and the cases are grouped into columns.[1] Cuneiform as a system of writing is practical only on clay: the characters are configurations of wedge-shaped traces impressed into the wet clay with a reed stylus, and with few exceptions, all record keeping, communication and literary transmission using cuneiform were done on clay. Cuneiform inscriptions *were* executed in stone and, to a lesser extent, in metal, wood and other materials for monumental or artistic purposes, although clay, too, could be used for commemoration, as can be seen from the texts in our dossier. The first three are on stone, but the remaining seven are on various types of clay artifacts (No. 10 also has a stone duplicate), only two of which are tablets of the usual sort. They will all be discussed in more detail shortly.

The form and material of the inscribed artifacts were closely linked to their function. Some royal inscriptions were intended for public display on monuments, such as the Stela of the Vultures (No. 2), erected to celebrate the accomplishments of a ruler. Many others, perhaps the majority of those preserved, were buried in the foundations or built into the walls of the structures whose building they commemorate, to be read only by the gods and by future rulers who might expose the inscriptions during reconstruction of the buildings. A third category of inscription was neither intended for public display nor completely hidden from view: objects presented to a deity for use in his temple. These could be inscribed, but unlike the stelas, whose primary function was to honor the ruler's greatness, the dedicatory inscriptions on votive objects were secondary to the objects' function in the cult, and the inscriptions were probably rarely read. Many of the inscriptions in our dossier neither commemorate the building of a temple nor accompany a votive offering, but celebrate the restoration to Lagash of territory that had been conquered by Umma, and thus form a rather anomalous group whose original context cannot be reconstructed.

One reason for this is that many (Nos. 2-4, 7-9) were found at Girsu before or just after the turn of the century, when archaeological technique was so primitive that many original contexts often went unnoticed. But perhaps there was little to notice: Nos. 1 and 5 were unearthed recently by the American expedition to Lagash, and both were found, reused as fill material, in constructions of later rulers. We are, at least, fortunate in knowing the provenience of most of the texts in our dossier. Only Nos. 6 and 10 are of unknown provenience; the rest are all from the sites of Girsu and Lagash. This, of course, means that our data represent just one side of the conflict. Our only piece of evidence presenting Umma's account is the fragmentary No. 10, which, as preserved, tells us little about Umma's version of the conflict, but what little there is suggests that that version would be a mirror image of the one we have from Lagash.

None of the texts in this dossier, then, are typical of the royal inscriptions of the epoch.[2]

---

[1] See the discussions of cuneiform and Sumerian in Kramer and in Oppenheim (Bibl. IA).
[2] See note 9 to Chapter I.

Whereas most such inscriptions go into great detail about a ruler's works, both pious and public, with less common summaries of military victories, our inscriptions have been chosen for their concern with the details of the boundary dispute between Lagash and Umma, a concern which in itself is rare among the surviving inscriptions. Only Nos. 1 and 5 resemble the usual inscriptions of the period.[3] No. 9 is not a royal inscription at all, but rather a literary text. Nos. 2, 6, 7, and 10 are unique and important documents whose significance will be discussed below.

Description of the Documents[4]

1. URNANSHE–STONE SLAB FROM LAGASH[5]

Found in the debris of a later temple, this is the work of an apprentice lapicide who was practicing his engraving technique on an already broken slab.[6] The obverse commemorates the building of the Bagar, Ningirsu's temple at Lagash, and continues with a report, typical of Urnanshe's other inscriptions, of the temples, canals and divine images constructed by him. The reverse contains the earliest extant account of the military success of a Sumerian ruler. Urnanshe introduces this account with the statement that he went to war against Ur and Umma, and then gives details of the victories individually. The naming of captured officers among the enemy troops is unique, and can be compared to the similarly unique bas-relief plaques with the figures of Urnanshe, his family and courtiers, in which each figure is labelled with the name and relation or title of the personnage it represents.[7]

2. EANATUM–BAS-RELIEF STELA (STELA OF THE VULTURES) FROM GIRSU[8]

The stela is reconstructed from seven fragments. On the obverse, the main scene shows the god Ningirsu holding a large net filled with enemy soldiers, reminding one immediately of the battle-nets of the gods that figure prominently in oaths that dominate much of the text. On the reverse, the main preserved scenes show Eanatum on foot leading a Lagashite phalanx, and Eanatum in a chariot at the head of a detachment of spearmen. At the lower left, a fragment shows the construction of a burial mound, which illustrates a phrase often found in these inscriptions in reports of military victories, that the victorious ruler made burial mounds of the enemy soldiers.[9] The stela is very possibly the one that Eanatum tells us, in col. xiii of the inscription, he erected in the temple of Ningirsu to commemorate his recovery of the Gu'edena from Umma.

The inscription itself is written in columns traversing the stela, interrupted frequently by the bas-relief, and is very fragmentary. This is especially unfortunate at the beginning, where we are given a detailed account of the Lagash-Umma border conflict, culminating in Eanatum's victory and restoration to the god Ningirsu of "his beloved field," the Gu'edena,

---

[3] A useful description of the style and structure of these inscriptions may be found in the introduction to *IRSA* (Bibl. IV).

[4] The numbers used here correspond to those given the translated inscriptions in Chapter VI, and are used throughout when referring to these inscriptions.

[5] *SARI* La 1.6, *ABW* Urn. 51; cf. Cooper, *Revue d'Assyriologie* 74,104ff.

[6] Cooper, *op. cit.*

[7] Strommenger (Bibl. ID), 73.

[8] *SARI* La 3.1, *IRSA* IC5a, *ABW* Ean. 1; illustrated in Strommenger (Bibl. ID) 66-69, Moortgat (Bibl. ID) 118-121, and here (partially), plates 1 and 2.

[9] E.g. Nos. 1 and 6 here.

which had been occupied by Umma. Embedded in this account is the story of the creation of Eanatum to be the super-human champion of Ningirsu, and the dream in which Ningirsu promises him victory. Following Eanatum's victory and a list of the fields restored to Ningirsu (agricultural tracts in ancient Sumer had names), Eanatum, in elaborate ceremonies, makes the ruler of Umma swear a series of similar oaths to the gods Enlil, Ninhursag, Enki, Sin, Utu and Ninki. Then Eanatum enumerates his titles, epithets and other victories, much as we find them in his other inscriptions. After a break in the text, he describes the erection of the stela to commemorate the restoration of the Gu'edena to Ningirsu, and tells us the stela's name (monuments and cultic objects, too, had names in ancient Sumer).

3. EANATUM–RIVER-WORN OVOID BOULDERS FROM GIRSU AND OF UNKNOWN PROVENIENCE[10]

These two boulders with identical inscriptions were ca. 25-30 cm. long in their unbroken states, and glorify the restoration to Ningirsu of "his beloved fields." The inscribing of river-worn stones is peculiar to the rulers of Presargonic Lagash, and their significance is unclear. One boulder commemorating the building of a temple by Enanatum I was associated with a copper peg-figurine bearing an identical inscription.[11] Since copper pegs formed part of foundation deposits, it has been suggested that the boulders, also, were buried in foundations of structures, though none have actually been so found.[12] That may have been true for some of the boulders (certainly for the Enanatum I boulder just mentioned), but these Eanatum boulders celebrate no building. And because one of them was found at Girsu itself, they could not have been intended to mark the new boundary with Umma, or be set in the foundation of any structure built in the reconquered territory.

The text begins with a short, fragmentary recapitulation of the boundary dispute, then catalogues the fields expropriated by Umma,[13] and reports the new names given to them (?) by the ruler of Umma. There follows a statement that Eanatum returned the fields to Ningirsu, respecting the original boundary marker.

4. EANATUM– CLAY VASE FRAGMENTS FROM GIRSU AND LAGASH[14]

These fragments of two inscribed vases recall immediately the larger and better preserved No. 10, the large clay jar containing one version of No. 6, and the fragments Nos. 11 and 12. Unlike inscribed stone vessels, which are valuable votive offerings to the deity, these clay vessels are not presented as offerings, but are merely the medium for the inscription, and the extant examples are restricted, with one exception, to those in this dossier, suggesting that the medium was used to honor political and military successes, rather than the building or restoration of temples and other works. Unfortunately, none have been found in contexts that provide any clue to their original emplacement.

The inscription, as restored, relates the original demarcation of the Lagash-Umma frontier, and the violation of the boundary by a ruler of Umma, followed by Eanatum's defeat of Umma and restoration of the original frontier. The inscription ends with a series of curses directed against any future ruler of Umma who might violate the border.

---

[10] *SARI* La 3.2, *ABW* Ean. 6.

[11] *SARI* La 4.5, *IRSA* IC6d, *ABW* En. I 27. The inscription is now duplicated on a stone tablet (Bibliotheca Mesopotamica 3, 1), which strengthens the connection with foundation deposits.

[12] Ellis, *Yale Near Eastern Researches* 2,119.

[13] Cf. the similar catalogue in No. 2 xv.

[14] *SARI* La 3.3, *ABW* Ean. 63 and Ent. 30.

5. ENANATUM I – CLAY TABLET FROM LAGASH[15]

This tablet, found in the temple of Hendursaga, was either a scribal copy or an archival record of a text which, according to the difficult final column, was inscribed on a copper standard in the temple. After enumerating the titles, epithets and religious constructions of Enanatum, the inscription relates the incursion by Urluma of Umma into the territory of Lagash, which he claims as his own. Encouraged by Ningirsu, Enanatum drives Urluma back across the border. The problematic outcome of the Enanatum-Urluma battle, as evidenced by the peculiar conclusion of the episode in this inscription, is discussed in Chapter IV. The final column, separated from the body of the inscription by a blank column, seems to be a notation specifying the locus of the original inscription and the object upon which it was inscribed. The mention of Enanatum's son Enmetena in this colophon suggests that the copy may have been made after the death of the former (IV.4).

6. ENMETENA – CLAY CONE AND JARS FROM GIRSU AND OF UNKNOWN PROVENIENCE[16]

This long inscription is completely preserved in two nearly identical versions, one inscribed on a cone similar to but finer than the famous cones of Uru'inimgina's Reform Texts (IV.6). The other is inscribed on a clay jar, and both are reported to have been found by the same member of a tribe in the Umma-Girsu area. A fragment of the end of the inscription is preserved on a piece of a broad-bottomed vessel from Girsu[17] (compare the inscribed vessel fragments discussed above). Like the inscribed vases, the large cones of Enmetena and Uru'inimgina are somewhat mysterious. Ellis thinks that they may have developed in imitation of the boulders (cf. No. 3),[18] but the form of the cones is very different. None have been found in a context that could provide a clue to their function. Like the inscribed vases, the texts of the cones are concerned primarily with political matters, and are quite different from the usual building and dedicatory inscriptions.

The inscription provides the most comprehensive preserved recitation of the boundary history, beginning with Mesalim's arbitration, and ending with Enlil and Ninhursag, the great god of Sumer and his consort, supporting Enmetena against a contemporary ruler of Umma who claimed part of the territory of Lagash. Enmetena then reconstructs the boundary-channel between Lagash and Umma, as well as the levee along the boundary channel. After a prayer for Enmetena, the inscription concludes with a curse against any future ruler of Umma who violates the border.

7. URU'INIMGINA – CLAY DISK FROM GIRSU[19]

This half-preserved disk is unusual both for its shape, and the manner of reading it, which is to read each column both on the obverse *and* reverse before going on to the next column (cuneiform tablets are generally read first entirely on one side, then on the other). Nothing is known of its original function.

The inscription, too, is unusual. It begins with a version of the famous Reform Texts of Uru'inimgina (IV.6), listing first the abuses of power, then the abolition of those abuses by decree of Uru'inimgina. There follows a history of the Lagash-Umma conflict, preserving

[15]*SARI* La 4.2, *ABW* En. I 29.
[16]*SARI* La 5.1, *IRSA* IC7i, *ABW* Ent. 28.
[17]The fragment was acquired by the Louvre with another fragment that has been joined to a third fragment excavated at Girsu (the two joined fragments are part of No. 4 here), so it is fairly certain that the fragment containing Enmetena's text was also found at Girsu.
[18]*Yale Near Eastern Researches* 2,117ff.
[19]*SARI* La 9.3, *ABW* Ukg. 6. The ruler's name was formerly read Urukagina.

only the episode concerning Enanatum I and Urluma. The inscription closes with a list of Uru'inimgina's pious construction activities. The inscription is unusual because neither of the two other preserved versions of the Reforms contain the history of the border conflict,[20] and because both other versions list Uru'inimgina's building activities at the beginning, which is where such a list would normally be expected (cf. Nos. 1, 5 and 8).

8. URU'INIMGINA—FRAGMENT OF A CLAY CYLINDER OR VESSEL FROM GIRSU[21]

The first preserved column of this small fragment of what was originally a very large artifact contains an account of Uru'inimgina's construction of a canal, well-known from other inscriptions of that ruler. The second and third columns contain fragments of an historical narrative which may or may not recount an attack by Umma on Lagash. It is included here to demonstrate how tantalizing and frustrating fragmentary inscriptions can be.

9. URU'INIMGINA—CLAY TABLET FROM GIRSU[22]

This inscription, which in some respects is a precursor of the later Sumerian lamentations over destroyed cities,[23] details the destruction wrought by Lugalzagesi of Umma on the territory of Lagash. It concludes by emphasizing that this was a transgression committed by that ruler, and was not provoked by any wrongdoing on the part of Uru'inimgina. The goddess of Umma, Nisaba, is asked to punish Lugalzagesi for his actions.

10. LUGALZAGESI—CLAY JAR AND STONE TABLET OF UNKNOWN PROVENIENCE[24]

The clay vase fragments which preserve well over half the original inscription, call to mind especially the vase fragments of No. 4, and the other pieces mentioned in the discussion of No. 4. The stone tablet, however, is a type of artifact most often associated with foundation deposits: a stone tablet and a copper peg-figurine bearing commemorative inscriptions were regularly buried in the foundations of temples being built or restored.[25] But this text commemorates no building, and the original placement of the vase and the stone tablet is a matter for conjecture. The stone tablet, perhaps, is the monument the ruler claims, in the inscription, to have erected to mark the border. Like the clay disk No. 7, the columns of the stone tablet are read on both obverse and reverse before moving to the next column.

The name of the ruler for whom the inscription was composed is broken, but it was almost certainly Lugalzagesi of Umma (and Uruk), the great king who claimed to rule over all of Sumer before he was defeated by Sargon of Akkad. This inscription is thus the only evidence from Umma for the Lagash-Umma border dispute. After enumerating the ruler's titles and epithets, we are told that he established the boundary of Umma, restoring the old markers. Then the text describes the border in detail, giving the distance

---

[20] See n. 23 for a suggested explanation of the historical portion.

[21] *SARI* La 9.4, *ABW* Ukg. 14.

[22] *SARI* La 9.5, *IRSA* IC11m, *ABW* Ukg. 16.

[23] Kramer (Bibl. IA) 38, 142ff., 208; *RLA* s.v. Klagelied. Sollberger (Bibl. II), 33ff. suggests that the trauma of the destruction recorded here led not only to this text's composition, but to a cycle of texts which could have included our Nos. 8 and 11, and perhaps No. 7 as well, which would explain why this last, unlike other versions of the Uru'inimgina Reforms, has a section recounting the history of the Lagash-Umma conflict. See also the interpretation of Westenholz (Bibl. II).

[24] *SARI* Um 7.2, *IRSA* IH2a, *ABW* Luzag. 2. Is the fragment *Oriental Institute Publication* 14,54 from Adab a duplicate (cf. Sollberger, *Orientalia* 28,344)?

[25] Ellis, *Yale Near Eastern Researches* 2,46ff.

between points along it. The ruler concludes the description by stating that he never transgressed the border, that he restored the old monuments marking it, and erected one of his own. The inscription ends with a curse against anyone who would violate the boundary.

11. NAME OF RULER NOT PRESERVED–CLAY VESSEL OR CYLINDER FRAGMENT FROM GIRSU[26]

This and the following fragment are included, as No. 8, to illustrate the problem of dealing with fragmentary texts. The mention of Umma in col. iii′ suggests this inscription belongs in our dossier, but unfortunately no royal names are preserved. The ultimatum of col. iv′ implies a whole new episode in the diplomatic exchanges between the two rival states, which is not attested elsewhere in the surviving inscriptions.

12. NAME OF RULER NOT PRESERVED– CLAY VESSEL FRAGMENT FROM GIRSU[27]

This fragment may suggest an alliance between Umma and Uruk in a joint struggle against Lagash (IV.6).

[26] *SARI* La 10.1, *ABW* AnLag 9; cf. note 23.
[27] *SARI* La 10.2, *ABW* LuTar v. Uruk I.

CHAPTER III

Difficulties in Reconstruction

The efforts of generations of scholarship are represented in section II of the bibliography. Despite these efforts and the abundance of our documentation, there is no general agreement on the details of the reconstruction of the border conflict between Lagash and Umma. The difficulties and disagreements involved are of three kinds: geographical, chronological and philological.

1. GEOGRAPHICAL PROBLEMS

The inscriptions and administrative documents from Presargonic Lagash have left us hundreds of place names and names of watercourses, yet only a small number can be identified with precision. Others can be put in the general vicinity of some known place, but the vast majority remain only vaguely situated at best. When, in text No. 6, Enmetena tells us that he constructed the boundary-channel between Lagash and Umma "from the Tigris to the Nun-canal," we may think we are in a position to trace that oft-disputed frontier, until we realize that we don't know where the Tigris *was* at the time[1]—it has shifted courses frequently—nor do we really know what is meant by the Nun-canal. Is it the arm of the Euphrates later known as the Iturungal, as shown in Map 2 (*RGTC* 1), or is it a branch canal that leaves the Iturungal at Zabala, as argued by Jacobsen and drawn by him on Map 3 (*Sumer* 25)?[2] In another inscription, Enmetena tells us that he extended the boundary-channel "from the Nun-canal to Mubikura."[3] If we combine the two passages, we can assume that Mubikura lies on the Tigris.

Now, administrative texts about a century later provide us with the following additional data:

1) The distance from the Nun-canal to Mubikura is ca. 53 km.[4]
2) The length of the boundary-channel from Munikura (assumed to = Mubikura) to bar-rá is ca. 48 km.[5]
3) The length of the Lagash boundary ending at the Nun-canal is ca. 58 km.[6]

All of this, when combined with Enmetena's testimony, suggests a boundary line of ca. 50-60 km. running from the Nun-canal to Mubikura on the Tigris. Yet even with this precision we have problems: "Assuming that the Tigris was the course of the present Duǧail, the distance of 53 km. of Mubikura on the Tigris to the Nun-canal would fit well with the identification of the Nun with the Iturungal. Assuming a more westerly course of the Tigris,

---

[1] "In fact, not a single settlement on the alluvium identified with the Tigris in pre-Hellenistic times can be identified that would permit the location of any part of the Tigris bed (or beds) to be specified" (Adams, Bibl. I A,158).

[2] Jacobsen, in any case, takes the just-quoted Enmetena passage to refer not to the traditional boundary-channel, but to another, new canal.

[3] *SARI* La 5.2, *ABW* Ent. 41.

[4] *RGTC* 1 s.v. Mubikura.

[5] *Ibid.*

[6] Falkenstein (Bibl. I B), 40 n. 3.

an identification of the Nun with the western Euphrates is conceivable."[7] And the whole question becomes even more complicated by the evidence of an Ur III text, more than 200 years later than Enmetena, that describes the Namnunda-field (the name of Enmetena's levee on the boundary channel is Namnunda-kigara "founded in Namnunda") as stretching from the Nun-canal to the Tigris, with an area that would allow the distance between the two waterways to be no more than 5 km.![8] The only solution that fits all the numbers is one that envisions a border beginning somewhere on the Nun-canal and running obliquely for 50-60 km. to the southeast between the Nun and the Tigris (a "western" Tigris, of course) 5 km. to the east, and joining the Tigris at Mubikura. This is very close to Jacobsen's border canal, the line on Map 3 from site 19 south to site 36, rather than to the east-west E-kisura ("boundary-channel") of Map 2 (*RGTC* 1).

There are also some philological reasons for favoring something like Jacobsen's solution. Text No. 6 speaks of "the boundary-channel of Ningirsu and the boundary-channel of Nanshe," which suggests—but does not demand—that the boundary ran from the territory of Girsu, city of the god Ningirsu, southeast to the territory of Nina, the city of the goddess Nanshe.[9] And finally, although the Lagash area has been the object of only a very preliminary archaeological survey,[10] both the results of that survey (Map 3), and Landsat imagery[11] support the notion of a northwest to southeast boundary canal, rather than one running east-west. But the tentative nature of the evidence supporting this conclusion must be stressed: no certain knowledge of the location of any place, river or canal mentioned in descriptions of the border; a philological argument based on the association of the boundary-channel with a goddess, which we assume means the ditch abutted territory belonging to that goddess's city; and traces of ancient canals provided by a very preliminary survey and inadequate Landsat imagery.

2. CHRONOLOGICAL PROBLEMS

The absolute chronology of the late Early Dynastic period can be roughly estimated by reckoning backwards from the relatively accurate dates for Mesopotamian rulers a millennium later. M. B. Rowton's contribution to the *CAH*[12] is an excellent demonstration of how this is done. A recorded solar eclipse in the reign of the Assyrian king Ashurdan III can be fixed to 763 B.C., and because we know the length of the reigns of his predecessors in Assyrian and Babylonia, we can reckon rather precisely back to the accession of Ashuruballit I in 1365 B.C.[13] A gap before this in our knowledge of rulers and lengths of reigns means that for the period earlier than ca. 1600 B.C., when we can again establish an unbroken chain of reigns, our absolute chronology is only approximate (but not in error by more than a century), even though the relative chronology is certain back to the beginning of the third dynasty of Ur, ca. 2100 B.C. Then everything becomes very doubtful. For the Presargonic period, we have inscriptions of nearly 60 rulers, but we can secure the length of

[7]*RGTC* 1 224.

[8] See the discussion of Pettinato (Bibl. II), 316ff.

[9] See already Poebel (Bibl. II), 227.

[10] Jacobsen (Bibl. II); cf. Adams (Bibl. I), 134.

[11] Adams (Bibl. I), 34, with the caveats on p. 33.

[12]*CAH* 1/1, 193ff.

[13]*CAH* 1/1, 202f.; Brinkman, *Analecta Orientalia* 43, 68.

reign for only the penultimate ruler of Lagash, Lugalanda (IV.6).[14] The Sumerian King List, to be sure, lists six or seven of the rulers attested in the primary sources, but attributes either unreasonably long reigns to them (Enmebaragesi of Kish, Mesanepada of Ur), or gives them suspiciously round-numbered reigns (25 or 30 years). The rulers of both Lagash and Umma, the protagonists of the historical reconstruction attempted here, are willfully excluded from the list, and other important rulers, such as Mesalim or Lugalkiginedudu are either excluded or present in broken portions of the list.[15] Essentially, we are reduced to reckoning by generations, rough estimates of average reigns and other even less reliable methods of approximation, all of which point to a period from about 2450-2300 for the time-span at Lagash from the accession of Urnanshe to the defeat of Uru'inimgina by Lugalzagesi.[16]

The relative chronology of the Lagash-Umma conflict is problematic in several instances. The texts never tell us how much time elapsed between the narrated episodes. Certainly each Ummaite violation could not have been as promptly punished as the texts would lead us to believe. The stages of the conflict between the primordial—for the texts—arbitration of Mesalim and the victory of Eanatum are compressed in texts Nos. 3, 4 and 6; in No. 2, they are told at length, but the inscription is badly broken. Thus, we are not certain whether Eanatum or one of his predecessors was the opponent of Ush, the first Ummaite foe mentioned in Enmetena's history of the conflict (No. 6). Eanatum's account of his struggle with Umma in No. 2 suggests that he had at least two major battles with that city, but the text is so poorly preserved that we cannot be certain. The internal chronology of Eanatum's reign is another problem: How are we to arrange the many victories and defensive battles he lists in his inscriptions, and where in his reign are we to situate his boundary settlement with Umma? When in Uru'inimgina's reign did the destructive raid by Lugalzagesi, described in No. 9, occur? Can this be correlated with the closing of the archive of the Emi at Girsu, and how long after that did Uru'inimgina continue to rule? These and other chronological problems will be discussed, if rarely resolved, in the reconstruction attempted in the following chapter.

3. PHILOLOGICAL PROBLEMS

There are still many Sumerian words whose meanings are unknown, and many more whose meanings have been only approximated. This is especially true for relatively early texts, such as the ones used in this study. Grammatically, too, Sumerian guards its mysteries; the nuances of the verb, for example, are notoriously recalcitrant to scholarly penetration. This is painfully obvious in the interpretation offered for the verb "to divert water" in No. 6. In view of the vulnerability of Lagash to any manipulation of the hydraulic system by its upstream neighbor Umma,[17] the most obvious way to understand the passages in

---

[14] We *may* know the length of the reigns of the two rulers before him; for the length of Uru'inimgina's reign, see IV. 6.

[15] Cf. n. 11 to Chapter I, and Piotr Michalowski's essay on the Sumerian King List in *Journal of the American Oriental Society* (forthcoming). The radical approach to the King List by Kammenhuber, *Orientalia* 48,1ff., is completely misguided.

[16] See the various reconstructions in the works in the Bibliography (IC), and note the shortening of the period from Sargon to Urnammu to under 200 years, which would be the result of accepting Hallo's convincing arguments in *RLA* 3,713f. The absolute dates given here, which follow the so-called middle chronology, may have to be set fifty years earlier, if Huber's just published endorsement of the high chronology is valid (Bibl. I).

[17] See Nissen (Bibl. III).

question is that Umma is diverting water out of the boundary-channel. But the verbal infix employed is most often interpreted as indicating action toward or into, and this interpretation seems to fit best in the broader context of these passages.

If the translations offered in Chapter VI were to reflect all of the uncertainties apparent to the Sumerologist, there would be many more blank spaces and question marks than there are. An attempt has been made to make the translations reasonable and readable. They have been made in the context of the reconstruction in Chapter IV, and while very aware that other reconstructions are possible, I have decided against an elaborate system of notation presenting all possible alternative translations and interpretations. These the reader can find in the works listed in the bibliography.

Not all of the problems are lexical or grammatical. The inscriptions are sometimes willfully elliptical; they just don't provide enough data to enable non-contemporaries like ourselves to understand what is being said.[18] The texts in Chapter VI are full of abrupt shifts and vague references that can only rarely be fleshed out from parallel or similar episodes in other texts. A passage in Eanatum's Stela of the Vultures (No. 2) tells us that "Eanatum, the man of just commands, measured off the boundary [with the leader of Umma?], left (something) under Umma's control, and erected a monument on that spot." What did he leave under Umma's control? We would be hard pressed to make sense of the passage without the fuller account given by Enmetena (No. 6): "Eanatum, ruler of Lagash, uncle of Enmetena ruler of Lagash, demarcated the border with Enakale, ruler of Umma. He extended the (boundary-) channel from the Nun-canal to the Gu'edena, leaving (a) 215 *nindan* (1290 m.) (strip) of Ningirsu's land under Umma's control, and establishing a no-man's land (there). He inscribed (and erected) monuments at that (boundary-) channel." How many other problematic passages, over which scholars continue to break their heads, would become intelligible if we had similar parallel accounts?

* * *

Geographical, chronological and philological problems such as those evoked above are barriers to reconstructing the history of the Lagash-Umma conflict as related in our dossier of contemporary inscriptions. It is only honest to stress, however, that even if all of these barriers were to be surmounted, the resulting history would be a very superficial one. The socio-economic, geo-political and religious realities of mid-third millennium Sumer are poorly understood. What really was a king? What was a border? Deceptively simple questions that are immeasurably more difficult to answer than are questions about a problematic passage or sequence of events. As historians of the ancient world, we operate in a continuous dialectical relationship to our own work and that of our colleagues. It is through the proposal and rejection of theses and modifications of hypotheses that our superficial history becomes more accurate, our real understanding more profound, and it is in this spirit that the following reconstruction is proposed.

[18] For the problem of textual silence on basic matters, see Civil, "Les limites de l'information textuelle," in Barrelet M.-T., *L'archéologie de l'Iraq*.

CHAPTER IV

The Border Conflict Reconstructed

1. BEFORE URNANSHE

Historical tradition at Lagash attributes the original arbitration of the Lagash-Umma border to Mesalim, the king of Kish generally thought to have lived about a century before Urnanshe, ca. 2600 B.C. (see Chap. I). Text No. 3 reports that "Enlil demarcated [the boundary between Ningirsu and Shara] and Mesalim erected a monument there," and that "Eanatum did not cross beyond the place where Mesalim had erected the monument." According to this same text, Eanatum carefully restored Mesalim's marker to its original spot on the boundary; text No. 4 says that he erected his own monument where Mesalim had erected one. Both acts are reported by Enmetena in his summary of Eanatum's reign (No. 6 ii). Enmetena also supplies us with the most complete account of the original arbitration:

> Enlil, king of all lands, father of all the gods, by his authoritative command, demarcated the border between Ningirsu and Shara. Mesalim, king of Kish, at the command of Ishtaran, measured it off and erected a monument there. (No. 6 i)

The boundary is represented as a matter decided by Enlil, chief of the Sumerian pantheon, between the gods Ningirsu and Shara, the chief deities of Lagash and Umma, respectively. In the world of men, Enlil's decision was carried out by Mesalim, whose hegemony extended to Umma and Lagash. So great was his prestige that his name was preserved, or considered worthy of mention, by the composers of our inscriptions over a century after the event, but the names of the local ruler of Lagash and his contemporary at Umma were forgotten or left unmentioned.

If the scribes of Lagash had forgotten the name of Mesalim's contemporary there, *we* know it. An inscribed and sculpted stone mace head from Girsu reads:[1]

> Mesalim, king of Kish, temple builder for Ningirsu, deposited this for Ningirsu. Lugalsha'engur is the ruler of Lagash.

We know nothing else about Lugalsha'engur. Another early ruler of Lagash, Enḥegal, who is called "king," is known only from an early land sale document.[2]

Eanatum's account in the Stela of the Vultures (No. 2) of the initial arbitration is broken, a pity because of the richness of detail it must have provided. When col. i picks up after the broken first twenty cases we read "He would pay it as a(n interest-bearing) [lo]an, and grain-rent was imposed on it." The text continues by introducing "the king of Lagash" before breaking off for 22 cases. When it picks up again, it tells of an act of defiance on the part of Umma, which is countered by Akurgal, Urnanshe's son and Eanatum's father. Since the 22 broken cases should suffice to cover Urnanshe, I would assign the reference to interest and grain-rent at the end of col. i not to Urnanshe's reign, but to the original settlement. The principle enunciated here is picked up again in the oaths sworn in the Stela of the Vultures (xviff.), and by Enmetena in text No. 6 ii, and is crucial, I think, to

---

[1] *SARI* Ki 3.1, *IRSA* IA3a, *ABW* Mes. v. Kiš 1.
[2] Edzard, *Sumerische Rechtsurkunden* No. 114.

an understanding of the entire conflict from Lagash's viewpoint. The cultivated area called Gu'edena (meaning "edge of the plains"), the territory claimed by both Lagash and Umma, the prize they fought over for countless generations, was, for Lagash, "Ningirsu's beloved field," as Eanatum never tires of telling us (e.g. at the end of Nos. 2 and 3). But G. Pettinato, in a long article that traces the conflict for two centuries beyond the period we are discussing, has shown that the Gu'edena was always divided between the jurisdictions of the two states (Bibl. II). The rationalization that allowed Lagash to accept the fact that part of the god Ningirsu's land was occupied by the forces of another god's city, was that this occupation was really a lease arrangement: Ningirsu's grain could be cultivated by Umma, but part of that grain was to be returned in the form of rent and interest.

In addition to making an unpleasant status quo palatable, this theoretical construct had some other advantages. When Lagash was strong, it might turn theory into fact and collect tribute from Umma. When, after a period of weakness, Lagash sought to regain part of the disputed territory from Umma, there was always a ready excuse to send ultimatums and finally resort to arms: Umma had failed to pay the requisite duties, or had exceeded its allotted acreage and transgressed the boundary.

2. URNANSHE AND AKURGAL

Until the recent publication of a stone slab found by the American archaeological expedition to Lagash (No. 1), we had no first-hand account of Urnanshe's military exploits. The typical Urnanshe inscription resembles the obverse of that slab: a long catalogue of temples built, statues fashioned and canals dug. Unlike such catalogues in later inscriptions from Lagash, he does not list the gods for whom these works were undertaken. On the slab's reverse, there is a unique report of successful battles against Ur and Umma. Again the style differs from later accounts. Urnanshe not only reports his victories, but gives us the names of important prisoners from each city. Later rulers of Lagash often tell us the names of other rulers they have defeated, but never the names of those rulers' subordinates.

The accounts of the two victories are interwoven in such a way as to suggest they may have been related. It will be argued below that from sometime before the reign of Lugalzagesi Uruk (-Ur) and Umma were allied and perhaps ruled by members of the same families, and that their control of most of the rest of Sumer was the major geo-political fact with which Lagash had to contend. The linking of Ur and Umma in Urnanshe's inscription may well be the earliest attestation of an alliance against Lagash between Umma and states to the southwest. The captured ruler of Umma, Pabilgaltuk, is otherwise unknown. The contemporary ruler of Ur is unmentioned, certainly because he remained uncaptured. But since the Meskalamdug dynasty at Ur had to precede the union of Uruk and Ur inaugurated by Enmetena's (junior?) contemporary Lugalkiginedudu and continued by his son Lugalkisalsi (IV.5), the ruler of Ur at the time of Urnanshe must have belonged to the Meskalamdug dynasty, and was possibly Meskalamdug himself.[3] The Meskalamdug dynasty, then, had interrupted the earlier dominance of Uruk in southern Sumer (p. 1), a dominance which was reestablished by Lugalkiginedudu.

When we pass from Urnanshe to the inscriptions of Eanatum and his successors, we enter a different world. Although Urnanshe mentions several captives from Umma by name, he never talks about the border as an object of contention. The Gu'edena, boundary-channels,

---

[3] Assuming a rough correspondence between the Lagash generations of 1) Urnanshe, 2) Akurgal, 3) Eanatum-Enanatum I, 4) Enmetena; and the generations at Ur of 1) Meskalamdug, 2) Akalamdug - Mesanepada, 3) A'anepada-Meskiagnuna, 4) Lugalkiginedudu. It is unlikely that this conflict of Urnanshe with a "leader" of Ur can be related to his small stela found at Ur; see n. 2 to *SARI* La 1.31.

and smashed monuments, all of which figure prominently in subsequent accounts of hostilities with Umma, do not occur in Urnanshe's account. Present evidence, including the general otherness of Urnanshe's inscriptional style discussed above, leads me to believe that the border conflict as a leitmotif in the historical records of Lagash, and the various topoi that accompany it, have their origin in the inscriptions of Eanatum. In the Stela of the Vultures (No. 2), "king of Lagash" at the end of col. i may well be the beginning of the Urnanshe episode in Eanatum's narration. By the time col. ii picks up after a 22 case break, Umma is defying Lagash, and Akurgal, Urnanshe's son and Eanatum's father, is introduced, but the text breaks off again. When it continues it is with another episode of defiance by Umma, and here it is clear that Umma is trespassing in the Gu'edena. This leads to Ningirsu's anger, which results in his creation of the larger-than-life Eanatum to be his champion (No. 2 iv-v). The implication is that the occupation of the Gu'edena that occurred under Akurgal remained for Eanatum to resolve. Some details of the occupation are preserved in No. 3: specific parts of the Gu'edena that were occupied are named, and the ruler of Umma apparently renamed them to commemorate his occupation.

An additional factor in Umma's invasion can be deduced from two difficult passages in the Stela of the Vultures, if they are properly translated here. Before actually battling the ruler of Umma, Eanatum curses him:

> The ruler of Umma—where is he recruiting?. With (other) men [. . .] he is able to exploit the Gu'edena, the beloved field of Ningirsu. May he (Ningirsu) strike him down!   (No. 2 vi)

Then, in a dream, Ningirsu predicts Eanatum's triumph in a passage that begins, "Kish itself must abandon? Umma, and being angry, cannot support it" (No. 2 vii). Umma, then, was not alone in its struggle against Lagash, but, as was probably the case during Urnanshe's reign (above), and *was* the case in the reigns of Enanatum I and Uru'inimgina (IV.4 and 6), it had powerful foreign allies.

In both Nos. 3 and 4 there is a telescoping of the events that were narrated in full on the Stele of the Vultures. After the initial boundary arbitration, the texts move on to the Ummaite invasion during Akurgal's reign that preceded Eanatum's recapture of the occupied territory. Both texts summarize the invasion in the same terms:

> [The leader of Umma] smashed that (Mesalim's) monument, and marched on the plain of Lagash . . . these (fields) the leader of Umma invaded? and smashed the monument. (No. 3)

> The leader of Umma smashed that [monume]nt and marched on the plain of Lagash. (No. 4)

Enmetena introduces the episode with a differently worded equivalent to the description of the haughty and defiant behavior of Akurgal's opponent in the Stele of the Vultures (No. 2 ii), and then continues exactly as Nos. 3 and 4:

> Ush, ruler of Umma, acted arrogantly: he smashed that monument and marched on the plain of Lagash. (No. 6 i)

The name of Akurgal's opponent, Ush (or Gish), is a new piece of information, that may have been in a broken section of the Stela of the Vultures. He was probably the successor of Pabilgaltuk, the ruler of Umma taken prisoner by Urnanshe (No. 1 r. iv).

3. EANATUM

The relative chronology of Eanatum's reign, which is of unknown length, cannot be disentangled, despite repeated scholarly efforts to do so.[4] His wide-ranging military activities

---

[4] Jacobsen (Bibl. III), 130ff.; Hallo (Bibl. III), 39ff.; Lambert, *Sumer* 8,71ff.

are most fully recorded in the following passages from an inscribed boulder commemorating the completion of the Lumagimdu canal:[5]

> Eanatum defeated Elam, the amazing mountain, and made burial mounds for it. He defeated the ruler of Urua, who stood with the (city's) emblem in the vanguard,? and made burial mounds for it. He defeated Umma and made twenty burial mounds for it. He restored to Ningirsu's control his beloved field, the Gu'edena. He defeated Uruk, he defeated Ur, he defeated Kiutu. He raided Uruaz and killed its ruler. He raided Mishime and destroyed Arua. All the lands tremble before Eanatum, the nominee of Ningirsu. Because the king of Akshak attacked, Eanatum, nominee of Ningirsu, beat back Zuzu, king of Akshak, from the Antasura of Ningirsu to Akshak, and destroyed it (Akshak).
>
> (report of the canal construction)
>
> Eanatum, who is commissioned by Ningirsu—to Eanatum, ruler of Lagash, Inana, because she loved him so, gave him the kingship of Kish in addition to the rulership of Lagash. Elam trembled before Eanatum; he drove the Elamite back to his own land. Kish trembled before Eanatum; he drove the king of Akshak back to his own land. Eanatum, ruler of Lagash, who subjugates the foreign lands for Ningirsu, defeated Elam, Subartu and Urua at the Suḫur-canal. He defeated Kish, Akshak and Mari at the Antasura of Ningirsu.

The first part of this summary appears nearly verbatim on other inscribed boulders,[6] and the assumption of M. Lambert that the second part, beginning with Inana's grant to Eanatum of the kingship of Kish (i.e. hegemony over northern Babylonia), is an elaboration of the first part, rather than a report of new engagements, is most plausible.[7] The repetition elsewhere of the first part suggests a fixed order of narrative, which is supported by the repetition, in the same wording and order, of selected victories in two other inscriptions.[8] Since the order is not geographic, it may be chronological, but this cannot be proved.

The only other inscription beside this one and those mentioned in notes 6 and 8 that details Eanatum's victories and conquests is the Stela of the Vultures, our No. 2. The narrative, spread over four columns (r. vi-ix) was originally extensive, but is mostly lost. The order and even the elements were *not* necessarily those of the inscriptions just discussed: Elam, Subartu [gap] Susa, Urua [gap] Arua, Sumer [gap] Ur [gap]. But the peculiar episode concerning Urua, and the verbs occurring with Arua and Ur *are* the same as in the other inscriptions. Clearly, many or most of the elements in Eanatum's historical narratives were fixed, and, as we have seen in the preceding paragraph, several inscriptions attest to one fixed ordering of those elements. The Stela of the Vultures shows that this order was not obligatory, and thus there is no way of knowing whether it was chronological or determined by other factors.

The account of Eanatum's struggle with Umma in the Stela suggests that there were at least two discrete episodes to the conflict. In col. xi, Eanatum is demarcating the boundary with Umma after the battle described in columns ix and x. But immediately following the demarcation, there seem to be new hostilities on the part of Umma, and before listing the fields that Eanatum restored to Ningirsu, the text tells us that Eanatum "destroyed the

---

[5] *SARI* La 3.5, *IRSA* IC5b, *ABW* Ean. 2. Many of these efforts, to be sure, are defensive, with Eanatum beating attackers back from Lagash's territory. But the actions against Uruaz, Mishime, Arua and Akshak are certainly portrayed as being offensive, and Eanatum could not have assumed the title "king of Kish" without having campaigned abroad.

[6] *SARI* La 3.6, *ABW* Ean. 3.

[7] M. Lambert, *op. cit.*

[8] *SARI* La 3.9, *IRSA* IC5c, *ABW* Ean. 22: The first three victories over Elam, Urua and Umma, and the defeat of Ur; *SARI* La 3.11, *ABW* Ean. 62: the defeat of Uruk and Ur (broken before and after, but traces before do not correspond to what precedes the defeat of Uruk in any other inscription).

foreign lands," either a reference to the victories to be described on the reverse, or to foreign allies of Umma. The implication is that there were at least two parts to the struggle with Umma. If the second confrontation came later in Eanatum's reign, and was commemorated by the Stela of the Vultures, it would solve one problem in the chronology of Eanatum: nearly all his inscriptions refer to a victory over Umma,[9] suggesting that that victory occurred early on, but the Stele of the Vultures, which commemorates a victory over Umma, has the long narrative of Eanatum's many foreign campaigns on the reverse, and thus could not have been fashioned near his reign's beginning. The lateness of the Stela is also suggested by the fact that only there, and in a tiny fragment of another inscription,[10] is Eanatum called "king" (*lugal*); in all other inscriptions his title is "ruler" (*ensi*).

There is yet another reason to believe that the Stela of the Vultures is later than the historical narrative on the boulders. The boulders imply that Kish in the broader sense (northern Babylonia; see Chap. I) was controlled by Akshak. It is after defeating Zuzu, king of Akshak, that Eanatum is granted the "kingship of Kish," and further on the text says that

> Elam trembled before Eanatum; he drove the Elamite back to his own land.

> Kish trembled before Eanatum; he drove the king of Akshak back to his own land.

The king of Akshak was the leading power in northern Babylonia, and we can presume that he also bore the hegemonist title "King of Kish" before it was assumed by Eanatum. But a cartouche on the Stele of the Vultures mentions an "Al[   ], king of Kish," certainly not Zuzu. A reasonable interpretation of this datum, in conjunction with the evidence for at least two wars against Umma discussed in the preceding paragraph, is that Al[   ] of Kish was defeated by Eanatum in a campaign that was distinct from, and later than, the expedition that ended in the defeat of Zuzu and inaugurated Eanatum's (temporary) hegemony over northern Babylonia.

The relatively meager and uncertain results of this discussion, as they bear on the Lagash-Umma conflict, are that Eanatum fought at least two wars with Umma over the Gu'edena. The first, near his reign's beginning, is mentioned in nearly all of his inscriptions. Another, rather later in his reign, was commemorated by the Stela of the Vultures.

The details of the first campaign proper against Umma are poorly preserved on the Stela, but the events leading up to it are well preserved and rather remarkable (No. 2 iv-viii). The god Ningirsu, angered at Umma's expropriation of his land, engenders the giant Eanatum, who is suckled by the goddess Ninḫursag and given his name by the goddess Inana. Eanatum utters an imprecation against the ruler of Umma, and then has a dream in which Ningirsu appears to him and predicts that Umma will lose its northern allies and will be defeated by Eanatum, after which the ruler of Umma will die at the hands of his own subjects. A fragmentary and difficult account of a battle follows, in which Eanatum appears to be wounded (No. 2 ix). Umma is defeated and Eanatum re-establishes the border, but fighting breaks out anew and Umma is vanquished once more (No. 2 x-xi). Following a fragmentary passage and the erection of a stela to commemorate his victory (presumably the Stela of the Vultures), the names of the parts of the Gu'edena restored to Ningirsu's (= Lagash's) control are enumerated (No. 2 xiii), after which begins a humiliating series of oaths that Eanatum forces the ruler of Umma to swear by the gods Enlil, Ninḫursag, Enki, Sin, Utu and Ninki (No. 2 xivff.).

---

[9] Only the short inscription *SARI* La 3.7 (*ABW* Ean. 5 and 8) does not; it mentions only Elam and Subartu.

[10] *SARI* La 3.12, *ABW* Ean. 64.

Each oath follows the same pattern: the ruler of Umma takes the battle-net of a particular god (see the illustration on the Stela itself of such a net, held by the god Ningirsu), and swears by that god that: 1) his use of land in the Gu'edena is as "a(n interest-bearing) loan;" 2) he will not do some untranslatable thing to the irrigation-channel (which served as a boundary line); 3) he will not trespass on Ningirsu's territory; 4) he will not alter the courses of the irrigation channels; and 5) he will not destroy the monuments that mark the border. He ends by calling down upon himself the very net by which he has sworn, if he ever violates the oath.[11] Eanatum then performs an obscure ceremony that entails releasing specially prepared birds toward the sanctuary of the god by whom the oath was taken, concluding with a curse against any future ruler of Umma who violates the oath.[12]

The reasons for assuming that the Stela of the Vultures and this elaborate ceremony commemorate a second victory of Eanatum over Umma later in his reign have been set forth above. It follows that the accounts of a victory over Umma given by Eanatum in texts Nos. 3 and 4 refer to an earlier campaign:

> Eanatum, ruler of Lagash ... restored to Ningirsu's control his beloved fields. Eanatum did not cross beyond the place where Mesalim had erected the monument, and (moreover) he restored that monument. (No. 3 iv)

> [Ningirsu] gave the order to Eanatum, and he destroyed Umma. At the [pla]ce where Mesalim had erected a monument, [E]an[at]um, [at Ningirsu's command, establish]ed a mo[nument]. When he thereby established the monument, [Eanatu]m [n]amed it "Ningirsu is the Lord Eternally Exalted in Abzu" (No. 4 ii)[13]

Both texts are less interested in Eanatum's military feats than with the fact that he re-established the ancient boundary of Mesalim. A similar concern about the border is expressed in Enmetena's report in text No. 6, but he also tells us something of Umma's defeat. After the transgression of Ush, which we placed in the reign of Akurgal (IV.2),

> Ningirsu, warrior of Enlil, at his (Enlil's) just command, did battle with Umma. At Enlil's command, he cast the great battle-net upon it and set up burial mounds for it on the plain. Eanatum, ruler of Lagash ... demarcated the border with Enakale, ruler of Umma. He extended the (boundary-) channel from the Nun-canal to the Gu'edena, leaving (a) 215 *nindan* (1290 m.) (strip) of Ningirsu's land under Umma's control, and establishing a no-man's land there. He inscribed (and erected) monuments at that (boundary-) channel and restored the monument of Mesalim, but did not cross into the plain of Umma. On the boundary-levee of Ningirsu, (called) Namnundakigara, he built a chapel of Enlil, a chapel of Ninḫursag, a chapel of Ningirsu and a chapel of Utu. (No. 6 i-ii)

Not only does Enmetena mention only one, not two, battles with Umma, but he makes the protagonist Ningirsu, leaving it to Eanatum only to draw the border after the war is over. The battle report, I think, is a summary conflation of Eanatum's struggles with Umma. The sequence of actors Ningirsu-Eanatum is nicely parallel to the sequence Enlil-Mesalim at the inscription's beginning, and the use of the divine battle-net echoes the oaths in the Stela of the Vultures as well as the curse at the end of No. 6.

The border settlement, however, is far from summary, and its detail enables us to understand an otherwise enigmatic statement in the Stela of the Vultures:

---

[11] The final oath, by the goddess Ninki, differs. Instead of a battle-net falling down upon the violator, snakes will rise up from the earth to bite him, and the ground will be pulled out from under him. See the note to the translation.

[12] These repeated oaths are somewhat reminiscent of the oaths in the much later vassal treaties of Esarhaddon, for which see the translation of E. Reiner in Pritchard, *Ancient Near Eastern Texts* (3rd ed.).

[13] This is the name of the monument replacing the original monument of Mesalim on the border, and has nothing to do with the Stele of the Vultures, which was erected in Ningirsu's temple at Girsu (No. 2 xiii), and was named "Ningirsu, the Lord, Crown of Luma, is the Life of the Pirigedena-canal" (No. 2 r. xi).

Eanatum, the man of just commands, measured off the boundary [with the leader of Umma?], left (some land) under Umma's control, and erected a monument on that spot. (No. 2 x-xi)

Without Enmetena's more explicit wording, the Eanatum passage would translate "left under Umma's control (literally 'to Umma's side')," not even telling us what was left. From Enmetena we know it was land, specifically a strip of land (as I interpret it) over one km. deep along the border, land that Enmetena tells us is Ningirsu's (i.e. belongs to Lagash), but is in Umma's control. It is this peculiar status that Enmetena describes as a "no-man's land" (literally "land without an owner").

Of all the rulers of Lagash known to us, Eanatum appears to have been the most wide-ranging in his conquests, and in the Stela of the Vultures, left us the grandest monument of the Early Dynastic period. Was his restoration of Ningirsu's Gu'edena to Lagash simply a restoration? His meticulous catalogue of tracts of land recovered, his repeated emphasis on restoration and insistence that he never went beyond the old Mesalim border markers, the humiliating series of oaths imposed on the ruler of Umma, the magnificence of the Stela of the Vultures itself—all these suggest that what Eanatum really did was not only to recover land occupied by Umma during the reign of his father Akurgal, but to annex lands that had traditionally belonged to Umma. But without testimony from the other side, this remains speculation.

4. ENANATUM I

There are three accounts from the inscriptions of three different rulers, of the hostilities between Eanatum's brother Enanatum I and Urluma of Umma. The events inaugurating the hostilities are told rather differently by Enanatum himself than by his son and successor Enmetena. Enanatum's version (text No. 5), a recent discovery of the American expedition to Lagash, occurs on a dedicatory inscription for the temple of Hendursaga, and the historical narration is relatively brief, concerned only with recording Enanatum's repulsion of Urluma's attempt to annex part of the territory of Lagash. The prelude to Urluma's invasion is simply "[when Enlil?] turned over control of Umma to [Nin]g[ir]s[u], and *he* then put it in Enanatum's control" (No. 5 vii). Enmetena's inscription is a detailed history of the border conflict, and is more concerned to give us the background to Urluma's invasion:

> The leader of Umma could exploit 1 *guru* (5184 hl.) of the barley of Nanshe and the barley of Nin-girsu as a(n interest-bearing) loan. It bore interest (in grain), and 8,640,000 *guru* (44,789,760,000 hl.) accrued. Since he was unable to repay? that barley, Urluma, ruler of Umma, diverted water into the boundary-channel of Ningirsu and the boundary-channel of Nanshe. (No. 6 ii)

Something similar, if more brief, must have been in the broken portion of No. 7 (Uru'inim-gina) just before it picks up with "Because of that barley . . ."

The conflict was clearly agricultural, involving payments for land use and improper use of irrigation systems. The Enmetena passage is the most elusive in our dossier, if not in the entire corpus. My interpretation follows, with some modifications, that of P. Steinkeller, *Journal of the Economic and Social History of the Orient* 24 143ff., and can only be regarded as tentative. The entitlement of Umma to the use of part of the Gu'edena in return for monetary and grain payments, is known from Eanatum (see above). Here, the amount of land it could use is stipulated as the acreage needed to produce 1 *guru* of grain. The next figure, 8,640,000 *guru*, is extraordinarily large, but in fact would be the amount of compounded interest that would accrue on 1 *guru* in about forty or fifty-five years at the current annual rate of 33 1/3 or 50 percent for grain loans and rent. The time-span could fit a period from early in Eanatum's reign to the end of Enanatum's reign, so there is no need to follow Steinkeller in drastically reducing the amount. However, the point of the figure

Plate 1. Eanatum Leading His Troops
(From the Stela of the Vultures, Photo Courtesy of the Musée du Louvre)

Plate 2. A Burial Mound Being Constructed for Fallen Ummaites
(From the Stela of the Vultures)

Plate 3. Enmetena "Cone" B
(Text No. 6; Photo Courtesy of the Yale Babylonian Collection)

Plate 4. The "Frontier of Shara"
(Text No. 10; Photo from *Orientalia* NS 28)

is its great magnitude, which underscores both the gravity of Umma's transgression and the justice of Lagash's cause.

Further on, when Urluma's successor Il invades Umma, he too diverts water and then "he _____ 3600 *guru* of Lagash's barley," for which action he is called a "field thief" (IV.5). The verb left blank is Sumerian *su*, the verb in the Urluma passage following the 8,640,000 *guru* and translated "repay"? is *sù*, and most scholars have assumed the same verb is meant in both instances. Steinkeller argues persuasively that *sù* and *su* are to be translated "to replace, repay," normally written *su*, but not infrequently *sù*.[14] No other possible meanings of *sù* ("to be/make distant, empty, to sprinkle") are appropriate in either passage, and another possible meaning of *su* "to sink, inundate" (later also written *sù*), makes no sense in the Urluma episode—he would not invade Lagash because he could not "flood" the grain. In the Il episode (see IV.5), "to flood" also does not fit the claims to Lagash's territory that follow the action.[15] Despite the awkwardness of "to repay" in that context, it is certainly the best solution that has yet been offered.

Urluma, then, was a delinquent debtor who compounded his transgression by diverting water into the boundary-channels and using them to irrigate land being exploited by Umma. That is, the boundary-channels were no longer considered to mark the border with Lagash, but were incorporated into Umma's irrigation network. The land they flowed through was treated as Umma's own. Later on, Urluma's successor Il does something similar: "He diverted water into the boundary-channel of Ningirsu and the boundary-channel of Nanshe," and for this he was called "the field thief" (IV.5).

The actual invasion by Urluma is described differently in our three sources, but with many of the same or similar elements, albeit not always in the same order:

> Urluma, ruler of Umma, [recruited foreigners?] and transgressed the boundary-channel of Ningirsu. "Antasura is mine! I shall exploit (its) produce?! " he said, and he awaited? him (Enanatum) at Du'urgiga. Ningirsu spoke ... angrily: "Urluma, ruler of Umma, has said, 'Antasura is mine!' and has marched on my very own field. He must not do violence against Enanatum, my mighty male! " Enanatum beat back Urluma, ruler of Umma, to the boundary-channel of Ningirsu. He went after him at the ... of the Lumagirnunta(-canal), and ... his garment. (No. 5 vii-xi)

> He set fire to their (the boundary-channels') monuments and smashed them, and destroyed the established chapels of the gods that were built on the (boundary-levee called) Namnundakigara. He recruited foreigners, and transgressed the boundary-channel of Ningirsu. Enanatum, ruler of Lagash, fought with him in the Ugiga-field, the field of Ningirsu. Enmetena, beloved son of Enanatum, defeated him. Urluma escaped, but was killed in Umma itself. He had abandoned sixty teams of asses at the bank of the Lumagirnunta-canal, and left the bones of their personnel strewn over the plain. He (Enmetena) made burial mounds in five places there for them. (No. 6 ii-iii)

> When, because of that barley, he (Enanatum I) sent envoys to him, having them say to him, "You must deliver my barley! ", Urluma spoke haughtily with him. "Antasura is mine, it is my territory! " he said. He levied the Ummaites and foreigners were dispatched there. At the Ugiga-field, the beloved field of Ningirsu, Ningirsu destroyed the Ummaite levies. He confronted the retreating Urluma, ruler of Umma, at the base of the Lumagirnunta-canal, and he (Urluma) abandoned his sixty teams of asses there, and left the bones of their pers[onnel strewn over the plain]. (No. 7 iv)

Enanatum reports Urluma's claim to the Antasura and vicinity as braggadocio in the midst of the invasion, whereas Uru'inimgina reports the same claim within the context of a diplomatic exchange (see Chap. V). Antasura, as we know, is, from Lagash's point of view,

---

[14] Steinkeller, *op. cit.*, n. 84.

[15] Note that in the one instance of crop destruction in our dossier, there is no mention of flooding (No. 9, end).

within the territory of Lagash very near to the border with Umma; but as we see here, it was claimed by Umma as its own (see also IV.5). The claim is omitted in Enmetena's account, possibly because he is saving his report of messages exchanged with Umma for the account of his own dispute with Urluma's successor Il.

The express claim by Urluma to Antasura seems to be a genuine detail specific to this episode; if it were just a stock phrase we would expect to find it in Il's declaration later on, but we do not. Another detail that the sources agree belongs only to this episode is the recruitment of foreign mercenaries or allies.[16] Note too, that Nos. 5 and 6 say that Urluma "transgressed the boundary-channel," whereas, e.g., the first invasion of Lagash by Umma was characterized in texts Nos. 3, 4 and 6 with the phrase, not otherwise used, "the ruler of Umma . . . marched on the plain of Lagash" (IV.2). The implications of this harmony among our sources will be discussed in Chapter V.

One note of discord is sounded by the name of the place of Umma's furthest advance. Whereas all three sources agree that Umma's ultimate disgrace was manifest at the Lumagir-nunta-canal, Nos. 6 and 7 put the initial battle with Urluma in the field named Ugiga, whereas Enanatum's own inscription sets it at a place called Du'urgiga, "hill of the black dog." Since the former is a very well known agricultural tract, and the latter hardly known at all, we can safely assume that the more common place name was substituted for the nearly homonymous, rarer one.

Our problem is less with the location of the battle than with its conduct and outcome. Enanatum (No. 5) tells us that *he* pursued Urluma to the Lumagirnunta-canal, but instead of using any of the well-attested Sumerian phrases that mean "to defeat," he expresses what he did to Urluma with an idiom involving a type of garment, so obscure that it is untranslatable.[17] According to both Enmetena (No. 6) and Uru'inimgina (No. 7), it was at this canal that Urluma ignominiously abandoned his chariotry and fled to his capital where, according to text No. 6, he was assassinated and replaced on the throne by his nephew. One could argue that Enanatum's dedicatory inscription to Hendursaga (No. 5) simply didn't have the interest or scope to relate such details, whereas Enmetena's inscription (No. 6), a history of the border conflict, did. But the fact that Enanatum does bother to detail the claims of Urluma to Antasura, and Ningirsu's angry reaction, suggests that if Urluma had got his comeuppance, we would have been told so in no uncertain terms. What is more likely is that things did not go well for Enanatum: Enmetena tells us that his father fought with Umma at the field Ugiga, but that he, "Enmetena, beloved son of Enanatum, defeated him." (No. 6). Already Poebel suggested that the absence of a royal title after Enmetena's name means that he fought under his father, who was still ruler. Perhaps, but the strange conclusion to the recently published No. 5, and its colophon which mentions Enmetena, taken together with Enmetena's own account, strongly imply that Enanatum was seriously, perhaps mortally, wounded in the battle, which was left for his son to conclude.

5. ENMETENA

Whether or not Enmetena defeated Urluma before or after formally inheriting his father Enanatum's office, it is reasonable to assume that his father did not long survive, if at all, the invasion of Urluma. Among the small number of dated documents from Enmetena's reign, the highest year number is 19, so he reigned at least that long. When, during his reign, did his confrontation with Urluma's successor Il occur? Evidence from Enmetena's activities on another front suggest that it was early.

---

[16] Possibly occurring outside this episode in No. 2 vi.
[17] See note 1 to No. 5.

To the southwest of Lagash, not far from the ancient metropolis of Uruk (see Chap. I), lies the town of Patibira (or Badtibira).[18] Large numbers of clay nails, some foundation tablets, a brick, and a copper peg figurine commemorate Enmetena's building of the temple Emush there. Of the three different inscriptions represented by these objects,[19] two contain important historical information. The text of the clay nails, which is extant in more copies than any other early Sumerian inscription, tells us, after the building report, that "at that time, Enmetena, ruler of Lagash, and Lugalkiginedudu, ruler of Uruk, established brotherhood."[20] In ancient diplomatic parlance, rulers who addressed each other as "brother" were on an equal level,[21] and this text had long been interpreted as the world's earliest evidence for a peace treaty or non-aggression pact. But its real meaning has been called into question by the recently published foundation tablet that tells us the following, after the building report:[22]

> He (Enmetena) cancelled obligations for the citizens of Uruk, Larsa and Patibira. He restored (the first) to Inana's control at Uruk, he restored (the second) to Utu's control at Larsa, and he restored (the third) to Lugalemush's control at the Emush (in Patibira)."

This can only mean that Enmetena had conscripted laborers for his construction of the Emush from Uruk and Larsa (just southwest of Patibira) as well as Patibira itself. Since it is unlikely that Enmetena did major work on the Emush more than once, the clay nails and this text must be contemporary. How then, could Enmetena and Lugalkiginedudu consider themselves equals, when Enmetena had the power to conscript citizens of Uruk?

Perhaps Enmetena's thrust to the southwest had reached Uruk or its vicinity, but then he pulled back to Patibira, recognizing the authority of Lugalkiginedudu west of there, and expressed this recognition by releasing conscripted citizens of Uruk and establishing "brotherhood" with Uruk's ruler. The reasons that Enmetena set his limit at Patibira cannot be determined from the extant evidence, but the person of Lugalkiginedudu himself must have had a lot to do with it. He would have negotiated his "treaty" with Enmetena, who calls him simply "ruler of Uruk," early in his career. Inscriptions by and for him found at Nippur and Ur say that he exercised "lordship in Uruk and kingship in Ur," and call him "king of Kish,"[23] all of which is inconsistent with a presence of Enmetena so close to Uruk at Patibira.

The best—if not the only—historical reconstruction that fits all of this evidence is the following: early in his reign, Enmetena successfully countered the claims of Umma, under Il, to part of the Gu'edena. He then turned to the southwest, and gained hegemony over a portion of Sumer[24] extending as far as Uruk, where he was resisted by Lugalkiginedudu.

---

[18] Crawford, *Iraq* 22, 197ff.

[19] *SARI* La 5.3 (*IRSA* IC7b, *ABW* Ent. 45), 5.4 (*ABW* Ent. 79), 5.5 (*ABW* Ent. 74).

[20] *SARI* La 5.3 (*IRSA* IC7b, *ABW* Ent. 45).

[21] See the same nearly contemporary usage at Ebla (Pettinato, Bibl. III, 96).

[22] *SARI* La 5.4 (*ABW* Ent. 79). See the long discussion by M. Lambert in the original publication of this text in *Rivista degli Studi Orientali* 47, 1ff. The duplicate stone tablet and figurine in Chicago are discussed by Biggs, *Revue d'Assyriologie* 69,185f.

[23] *SARI* Uk 1.1 (*IRSA* IE1c, *ABW* Lukin. v. Uruk 2), 1.2 (*IRSA* IE1d, *ABW* Lukin. v. Uruk 4), and 1.6 (*IRSA* IE1b, *ABW* Lukin. v. Uruk 3). The title in this last inscription (*UET* 1,3) had previously been read "king of Umma," but a collation made at the suggestion of A. Westenholz reveals "Umma" (ŠÁR x DIŠ) to be the beginning of the sign KIŠ.

[24] Note the dedication by him of a vase in the temple of Enlil at Nippur (*SARI* La 5.18, *ABW* Ent. 32). The statue of Enmetena found at Ur (*SARI* La 5.17, *IRSA* IC7a, *ABW* Ent. 1) commemorates the building of a temple for Enlil in the Lagash area, and must have been brought to Ur in antiquity as a result of a raid or antiquarian foraging. It cannot be used as evidence for Enmetena's rule in Ur.

The establishment of "brotherhood" recorded on the Patibira clay nails represents a coming to terms with that resistance. Lugalkiginedudu went on to reassert the hegemony of Uruk over southern Sumer, after a period of dominance by Ur under the Meskalamdug dynasty, and then extended his hegemony northward to Nippur, and into northern Babylonia. The influence of Lagash must have shrunk accordingly.[25] There is no way to know the extent to which this expansion of Uruk overlapped Enmetena's reign, or how much of Lugalkiginedudu's career extended into the reigns of Enmetena's successors.

We have only one source for the Lagash-Umma border dispute during the reign of Enmetena, a long history of the conflict written during the reign of that ruler himself:

> At that time, Il, who was the temple-estate administrator at Zabala, had marched in retreat from Girsu to Umma. Il took the rulership of Umma for himself. He diverted water into the boundary-channel of Ningirsu and the boundary-channel of Nanshe, at the boundary-levee of Ningirsu in the direction of the bank of the Tigris in the region of Girsu, the Namnundakigara of Enlil, Enki and Ninhursag. He repaid? (only) 3600 *guru* of Lagash's barley.
>
> When, because of those (boundary-) channels, Enmetena ruler of Lagash, sent envoys to Il, Il ruler of Umma, the field thief, speaking in a hostile way, said: "The boundary-channel of Ningirsu and the boundary-channel of Nanshe are mine! I will shift the boundary-levee from Antasura to Edimgalabzu," he said. But Enlil and Ninhursag did not allow him (to do) this.
>
> Enmetena, ruler of Lagash, nominee of Ningirsu, at the just command of Enlil, at the just command of Ningirsu, and at the just command of Nanshe, constructed that (boundary-) channel from the Tigris to the Nun-canal. He built the foundations of the Namnundakigara for him (Ningirsu) out of stone, restoring it for the master who loves him, Ningirsu, and for the mistress who loves him, Nanshe. (No. 6 iii-v)

Zabala was an important cult-center of the city-state Umma (as, for example, Girsu was part of Lagash), and Il, whom we know from inscriptions as Urluma's nephew, was part of the Ummaite force that invaded Lagash. When his uncle was killed (IV.4), Il succeeded his uncle as ruler in Umma. The actions of Il that precipitated his conflict with Enmetena have been interpreted together with the similar actions taken by his predecessor Urluma in the reign of Enanatum (IV.4): He utilized the boundary irrigation-channels and hence exploited the border lands of the Gu'edena for Umma's benefit, but only paid a fraction of what was owed Lagash for their use. Whether Umma still owed Lagash the enormous sum mentioned in the Urluma episode is unclear, and the awkwardness of the translation "He repaid? (only) 3600 *guru* of Lagash's barley" has been noted in IV.4. But whatever the uncertainties of interpretation in this section may be, what immediately follows is clear: Enmetena sent envoys to Il "on account of those (boundary-) channels," in my interpretation because Il had incorporated the channels and the territory they watered into his domain, and is thus called a "field thief." Il claims the boundary-channels, and announces his intentions to shift the boundary-levee from Antasura to Edimgalabzu. Whereas the phrase "I will shift the boundary-levee" depends on a slight emendation of an otherwise unintelligible phrase—which does not guarantee the correctness of the emendation—the phrase "*from* Antasura *to* Edimgalabzu" is not to be disputed. Antasura, whence Eanatum beat back the enemies of Lagash (IV.3), to which Urluma of Umma laid claim (IV.4), the second sanctuary destroyed by the forces of Lugalzagesi (No. 9 i), is a symbol of the frontier with Umma. Edimgalabzu, a settlement in the Gu'edena, is the midpoint on the border that Lugalzagesi imposed on Lagash according to text No. 10:50ff. Thus my interpretation is that Il is proclaiming his intention to annex Antasura and move the boundary forward, into Lagash's territory, to Edimgalabzu (as Lugalzagesi successfully did a few generations later).

---

[25] For a very different interpretation of these events, see M. Lambert, *Oriens Antiquus* 20,176f.

The conclusion to this confrontation with Il of Umma is decidedly unmilitary. Does "Enlil and Ninhursag did not allow him (to do) this" imply that Il meekly withdrew once his bluff was called, or is it a euphemistic expression of Enmetena's inability to enforce the claims of Lagash? It has been argued above that this episode probably occurred early in Enmetena's reign, before his confrontation with Lugalkiginedudu. Since Enmetena's hegemony soon extended all the way to Patibira, it is unlikely that it was he who backed off in a confrontation with nearby Umma.

The new or extended boundary-channel built by Enmetena at the conclusion of this confrontation has been discussed in III.1. To summarize the discussion there, we are unsure, to begin with, where either the Nun-canal or the Tigris of that period were. Several texts indicate that the distance of the new boundary-channel should be 50-60 km., but another text tells us that the distance between the Nun and the Tigris is no more than 5 km. Both can be true, the crucial and unknown bit of information being *where* on the Nun-canal the channel began, and *where* on the Tigris it ended. The currently available data support the notion of a boundary-channel taking off somewhere on the Nun-canal and running obliquely for 50 or so km. between the Nun and the Tigris, to a point on the latter wherever the settlement Mubikura was located.

6. URU'INIMGINA

We know next to nothing about the external relations of Lagash between the time of Enmetena and the destruction caused by Lugalzagesi, reported in text No. 9. A letter to Enentarzi, the temple-estate administrator (*sanga*) at Girsu, from Lu'ena, his colleague at Ninmarki, reports the interception of an Elamite raiding party, and is dated to the fifth year of the reign of Enanatum II, the son and successor of Enmetena (Chap. I). If, as Grégoire has tried to show, Enanatum II was killed in that raid,[26] then his reign lasted no more than five years, but this is uncertain. His successor was Enentarzi, the Girsu temple-estate administrator. Following the examples of Umma and Zabala, where Il, the temple-estate administrator at Zabala succeeded his uncle Urluma on the throne of Umma (IV.5), M. Lambert has suggested that Enentarzi and his predecessor as temple-estate administrator, (possibly his father) Dudu, were junior members of the royal family.[27] Others assume that with the demise of Enanatum II, the dynasty founded by Urnanshe came to an end.

Enentarzi was ruler for at least, and probably only, six years, and Lugalanda, possibly his son, followed him for seven years before the advent of Uru'inimgina.[28] During the eighteen or more years from the accession of Enanatum II to the accession of Uru'inimgina we must still take into account the continued dominance of Uruk over most of Sumer. This had been established by Lugalkiginedudu during Enmetena's reign, and continued under the former's son Lugalkisalsi.[29] Inscriptions from Nippur and Uruk testify to the reign of Enshakushana, son of Elilin, who styled himself "lord of Sumer and king of the Land," was

[26] Grégoire (Bibl. III) 11.

[27] *Rivista degli Studi Orientali* 47,101ff.

[28] The name was formerly read Urukagina. For the new reading, see Bauer (Bibl. III), 65; W. Lambert, *Orientalia* 39, 419.

[29] Nissen (Bibl. IC), 125; Falkenstein (Bibl. IB), 124 n. 1. Both refer to a passage by Gudea of Lagash (ca. 2150 B.C.) that mentions a stela of Lugalkisalsi set up in the temple of Ningirsu at Girsu, which would suggest the temporary dominance of that ruler over the state of Lagash, unless the stela was booty that had at some time been brought to Lagash after a successful raid. Edzard, *Compte Rendue* de la 20ème Rencontre Assyriologique Internationale, p. 161, however, interprets the Gudea passage differently.

"king of Uruk," and boasted of a victory over Kish.[30] We know that he could not have
ruled too much earlier than Sargon,[31] and so must have followed Lugalkisalsi. Unfortunately, perhaps two other rulers of Uruk must be squeezed into the time between Lugalkisalsi and the last king of Presargonic Uruk, Lugalzagesi: Urzage, known from a legal
document and an inscription from Nippur, where he uses the title "king of Kish,"[32] and
Lugal-TAR in text No. 12. Both may, however, have preceded Lugalkiginedudu.

From Umma, we have a gold plaque commemorating the building of a dais for Shara,
head of the pantheon of Umma, by Bara'irnun, wife of Gishakidu king of Umma.[33] Gishakidu was the son, and presumably successor, of Il, the ruler of Umma whose challenge to
Enmetena was frustrated by the gods (IV.5). Lugalzagesi, in his great dedicatory inscription
from the Enlil temple at Nippur, reports that he is the "king of Uruk and king of the
Land . . . son of U'u ruler of Umma."[34] We cannot tell if U'u was the immediate successor
of Gishakidu, or if they were of the same dynasty. But Lugalzagesi is clear that his father
was ruler of *Umma*, which means either that Lugalzagesi, scion of Umma's ruling family,
widened his city's hegemony to include Uruk and Ur, and most of the rest of Sumer, or that
there had already been a close relationship between the ruling families in both Umma and
Uruk; perhaps they were the same family. In the notes to No. 12, I suggest that, if correctly
restored, that inscription might point to an alliance, if not a closer connection, between
Umma and Uruk against Lagash. And earlier, we have seen evidence for a possible alliance
between Ur and Umma against Lagash (IV.2). There is, therefore, reason to view the rule of
Lugalzagesi of Umma in Uruk, in the tradition of close ties between Umma and Uruk (-Ur),
rather than as an innovation arising from conquest.

In the catalogue of Umma's destruction in Lagash (No. 9) Lugalzagesi is called "ruler of
Umma." But M. Lambert[35] and B. Hruška[36] cite documents that bear on the reconstruction
of Lugalzagesi's reign: from Uru'inimgina's year 4, a reference to an expenditure made
"when the leader of Uruk besieged the city," and from year 6, a month characterized as
"when the leader of Uruk came a third time." These immediately recall text No. 8 iii'
"[he] besieged? Girsu. Uru'inimgina battled him and . . . its (Girsu's) wall. . . . He returned
to his city, but [he] came a second time [. . .]." There are two possibilities: The "leader
of Uruk" is Lugalzagesi, already ruling at Uruk, and these data as well as No. 8 refer to the
prolonged conflict between him and Uru'inimgina.[37] Or, we might think of text No. 12,
which refers to a "Lugal-TAR, ruler of Uruk" as a seeming adversary of Lagash who is

---

[30] *SARI* 4.1 (*IRSA* IH1b 1-26, *ABW* Enšak. v. Uruk 1 and 3), 4.2 (*IRSA* IH1b 27-31, *ABW* Enšak. v.
Uruk 2), 4.3 (*ABW* Enšak. v. Uruk 5). His father Elilin may be the same as Elili, "king of Ur," known from
an inscription from Eridu (*SARI* Ur 8, *IRSA* IB7a, *ABW* Elili v. Ur 1), who, in turn, may be identical
with Elulu of the first dynasty of Ur in the Sumerian King List.

[31] Westenholz, *Bibliotheca Mesopotamica* 1, p. 4.

[32] M. Lambert, *Revue d'Assyriologie* 73,1ff.

[33] *SARI* Um 6, *IRSA* ID5a, *ABW* Giš. v. Umma 1.

[34] *SARI* Um 7.2, *IRSA* IH2b, *ABW* Luzag. 1. That he does not call himself "king of Kish" is instruc-
tive, and suggests that his hegemony never extended much beyond Nippur. The references in the inscription
to foreign lands extending as far as the Mediterranean Sea certainly refer to foreign trade not to conquest or
control (Chap. I). Note that in this inscription, when Lugalzagesi specifies the cities that prospered from his
rule, he mentions only Uruk, Ur and Larsa—cities of the old Uruk-Ur union (IV.5)—and Umma with its
satellites, Zabala and Kidingir.

[35] *Rivista degli Studi Orientali* 50,32f.

[36] Hruška (Bibl. III), 160.

[37] See M. Lambert, *Rivista degli Studi Orientali* 50, Hruška (Bibl. III) and Sollberger (Bibl. II) for other
evidence culled from the administrative documents of Uru'inimgina's reign that attests to a protracted and
debilitating (for Lagash) period of hostilities, and note Westenholz's remarks (Bibl. II) on events immediately preceding those hostilities.

sending troops (against Lagash?) for "a tenth time." Even *if* the "leader of Uruk" of the administrative documents is not Lugalzagesi, but Lugal-TAR or someone else, given the hypothetical long-term Uruk-Umma relationship proposed above, the siege and attack referred to in the documents could still be part of the same hostilities that culminated in the destruction described in text No. 9.

The circumstances of Uru'inimgina's accession to rulership are unclear. Nowhere does he refer to his father, and he tells us that "Ningirsu, warrior of Enlil, granted the kingship of Lagash to Uru'inimgina, selecting him from among the myriad people."[38] In both respects, he finds a parallel in Gudea, nearly 200 years later, who, if not in direct line to the throne, did belong to the royal family.[39] Enmetena, too, tells us he was chosen from among the myriad people,[40] and *his* father was the ruler Enanatum I. Uru'inimgina's predecessor Lugalanda was apparently dead by the former's second year,[41] which could indicate either that his natural death led to Uru'inimgina's orderly succession, or that he was killed in some sort of upheaval during or after which Uru'inimgina seized power. Lugalanda's wife, in any event, received an elaborate state funeral when she died in Uru'inimgina's third year, which means that the former ruler could not have been completely discredited.[42] However, there is a good chance that socio-economic tensions that found expression in Uru'inimgina's famous "Reforms," when he "replaced the customs of former times," led to the change of rulers. The meaning of those Reforms is still being hotly debated, and further discussion here would add nothing to our investigation of the Lagash-Umma conflict.[43] Note only that one version of those Reforms contains an historical summary of that conflict (No. 7).

If the assumptions made in earlier paragraphs are correct, then Lagash at this time was under pressure from a Sumer united under the leadership of Uruk, which leadership had strong, possibly familial ties to the local ruler at Umma. It is not impossible that Lugalzagesi was functioning in both capacities,[44] but he was certainly already in power at Umma early in Uru'inimgina's reign. The conflict with Uruk-Umma is reflected in the references to the "leader of Uruk" in the administrative texts cited above, in text No. 8 and possibly No. 12. The devastation described in No. 9 represents a climax to these hostilities, but the fact that the text could be written, and that Uru'inimgina is mentioned in it as king, means that the destruction was not total, and probably that Uru'inimgina survived, master of a considerably smaller realm. The new border, drawn by Lugalzagesi in text No. 10, has as its midpoint (presumably controlled by Umma) Edimgalabzu, long a possession of Lagash that had been unsuccessfully claimed by Umma as early as the reign of Enmetena (IV.5).

No. 9, as only two other inscriptions,[45] calls Uru'inimgina "king of *Girsu*," not Lagash. This fits well with the contents of the tablet, which lists among the sanctuaries destroyed

---

[38] *SARI* La 9.1 vii (*ABW* Ukg. 4). The reference here to "kingship" marks the fact that Uru'inimgina, in his second year, dropped the title "ruler" (*ensi*) that had been used by his predecessors, and assumed the title "king" (*lugal*) that had not been used in Lagash since the reign of Eanatum (IV.3).

[39] Falkenstein (Bibl. II), 1ff.

[40] *SARI* La 5.18 (*ABW* Ent. 32). The context is broken.

[41] Bauer (Bibl. III) 96.

[42] See Sollberger (Bibl. II), 31, (Bibl. III), 33f., and Rosengarten (Bibl. III), 184f. n. 3.

[43] The Reform Texts are *SARI* La 9.1 (*ABW* Ukg. 4), 9.2 (*ABW* Ukg. 1) and 9.3 (*ABW* Ukg. 6 = No. 7 here). For the latest discussions of the Reforms, including a summary of earlier interpretations, see Maekawa (Bibl. III) and Foster (Bibl. III). See also Hruška (Bibl. III), Edzard (Bibl. III) and Sollberger (Bibl. III). A new translation and interpretation is being prepared by Gelb and Steinkeller.

[44] Support for the notion that Uruk and Umma were being governed together, but under separate titular leadership, comes from the inscription cited in n. 17 to Chapter I.

[45] *SARI* La 9.2 (*ABW* Ukg. 1) and 9.13 (*ABW* Ukg. 58).

by Lugalzagesi cult-places outside, but close to, Girsu near the border (Ekibira, Antasura, Tirash), and continues with cult-places that, when they can be localized, are in the Lagash and Nina area. Thus, Girsu proper seems to have been spared, and Uru'inimgina's realm was restricted in his title to that city only.[46] The events of text No. 9 are usually correlated with the cessation of administrative documents in Uru'inimgina's seventh year. These documents, nearly 1600 altogether, which span the reigns of Enentarzi, Lugalanda and Uru'inimgina (through his seventh year), belong to the archive of the Emi, the organization (temple-estate) that administered the properties controlled by the ruler's wife.[47] The texts were nearly all found by clandestine diggers and disposed of through antiquities dealers, and while Girsu is their presumed provenience, we have no idea where the archive was actually found. Possibly it was in a part of Girsu outside the city-walls, but separately enclosed, that *was* affected by Lugalzagesi's raid of text No. 9, which would explain the archive's sudden cessation in Uru'inimgina's seventh year.[48] Or, we may have a storage archive, covering a specific time period, rather than an active archive. In that case, the cessation of records in Uru'inimgina's seventh year would have no meaning other than an administrative one, unless that particular year was chosen to close the archive just because of disruptions caused by the raid described in text No. 9. Be that as it may, the latest documented year of Uru'inimgina is his eleventh,[49] known from a clay tag found at Girsu[50] commemorating some landscaping he donated to a sanctuary. How much longer he exercised authority is not known; we know only that under Sargon's son Rimush, someone else was *ensi* at Lagash, and under Rimush's successor Manishtushu, Uru'inimgina had a namesake in a son of another *ensi* of Lagash.[51]

7. CONCLUSION

The preceding narrative of the Lagash-Umma conflict is not a history. In harmonizing the obviously one-sided accounts from Lagash itself, I have tried to reconstruct the historical tradition of the conflict at Lagash, as it circulated among the scribes who drew on it to compose the inscriptions of their employers (see Chapter V). Only occasionally have I been able to pick up on certain clues—an awkward phrase, a too-vehement protest—to suggest that the picture was other than the scribe painted it. Rarely, evidence from outside Lagash, such as the inscriptions of Lugalkiginedudu or Lugalzagesi, could be utilized to broaden the perspective.

The conflict, as portrayed, is about land, more specifically the Gu'edena, a territory that was always divided between Umma and Lagash. Beginning with Eanatum, a border supposedly fixed generations earlier by Mesalim of Kish was invoked to support the claims of Lagash: Umma's rights in the Gu'edena were limited and to be paid for. For its part, Umma asserted its own counter-claims at every opportunity, known to us unfortunately only through texts of the enemy. The whole conflict was played out within a wider geo-political framework, in which Lagash seems to be engaged in a struggle for hegemony in southern Babylonia with Uruk and Ur, united at least since the time of Lugalkiginedudu, and Umma, often, if not always, allied with Uruk and Ur. This broader conflict could not

---

[46] For the chronology of Uru'inimgina and his survival beyond his seventh year, see Sollberger (Bibl. II).
[47] See Maekawa (Bibl. III).
[48] M. Lambert, *Rivista degli Studi Orientali* 31,141, put the archive as far away as Nina, and says it was brought to Girsu for safekeeping after the attack of Lugalzagesi, but his reasoning is not persuasive.
[49] The tenth year of his kingship; see n. 38.
[50] *SARI* La 9.14d (*ABW* Ukg. 38). From its Louvre accession number, it belongs to the objects from de Sarzec's excavations, long before the archival texts appeared on the market.
[51] Sollberger, *Archiv fuer Orientforschung* 17,29.

but exacerbate the local conflict, but *only* a long-standing conflict with a close neighbor could evoke the bitterness, outrage and indignation evident in many of these inscriptions. The triumph of Lugalzagesi, witnessed by texts Nos. 9 and 10, which closes our account of the conflict, only marks a pause, not a conclusion, to a struggle that would continue for centuries.[52]

[52] See Pettinato (Bibl. II).

CHAPTER V

Historical Tradition and the Language of History

Of what did the "historical tradition" mentioned in the last chapter's conclusion consist? We have seen, when examining the different episodes of the Lagash-Umma conflict, that many of the same or similar phrases recur in the narration of a given episode, not only in different inscriptions of the same ruler, which would not be surprising, but in inscriptions of different rulers as well. Perhaps the clearest illustration of the tradition's maintenance of specific vocabulary for specific episodes is in the distinction between the invasion of Ush, who "marched on the plain of Lagash" (IV.2), and the invasion of Urluma, who "transgressed the boundary-channel" (IV.4). Other examples include the memory of Mesalim's demarcation of the boundary and Eanatum's restoration of Mesalim's stela (IV.1 and 3), the notion that Umma must compensate Lagash for use of the Gu'edena (IV.3), and Urluma's abandoned charioteers (IV.4). At other times, we have seen conflicts between versions of episodes, such as the place of Enanatum's initial contact with Urluma (IV.4), explained as the substitution for a rare toponym of a nearly homonymous common one, or in the eventual outcome of that contact, which betrays an unspoken unhappy ending (IV.4). We have also seen occasional differences in sequences and emphasis, as well as ellipses that we understand only by reference to the fuller version of another text (III.3). But the overall impression is one of a consistent, unified tradition, drawn upon by the composers of the inscriptions, beginning with Eanatum.

Assyrian annals or Babylonian chronicles are at least a millennium away.[1] Year names were not used by the rulers of Lagash, and the information provided by lists of such names, even in their fullest form, could not have been a source for our scribes' historical knowledge and phraseology.[2] The colophon to text No. 5 suggests that copies of monumental inscriptions were kept in archives, and perhaps these were available to the composing scribes. Or perhaps a standardized history was learned by rote.

We have nothing that could have been the source for the inscriptions' historical sections. The Stela of the Vultures (No. 2), elaborate as it was in its unbroken state, cannot be the source of Enmetena's account of the border Eanatum drew with Enakale of Umma, since Eanatum's elliptical description of the land left under Umma's control is intelligible only from Enmetena's fuller version (III.3). In the Urluma-Enmetena episode of the conflict (IV.4), Uru'inimgina's account of Urluma's invasion and defeat (No. 7 iv) varies with Enmetena's (No. 6) against Enanatum's (No. 5) by giving the site of the original clash as the field Ugiga, rather than Du'urgiga. Uru'inimgina also recounts in terms identical to No. 6 Urluma's abandonment of his chariotry.[3] But lest we imagine that No. 6 is the source of No. 7's account, notice that Urluma's claim to the Antasura is absent in No. 6 (Enmetena's inscription), but *can* be found in both No. 5 (Enanatum) and No. 7

---

[1] Grayson, *Orientalia* 49,150ff. (annals) and 173f. (chronicles).

[2] The most common form of dating in the late third and first half of the second millennia was to name a year after an important event. A list of such year names would thus constitute a sequence of notable events in the reign of a particular ruler (see e.g. Pritchard, *Ancient Near Eastern Texts* [3rd ed.] 296ff.).

[3] The topos of abandoned troops, this time captured rather than slain, recurs in the fragment No. 12.

(Uru'inimgina). If Uru'inimgina's scribes were relying on a text of Enmetena for their information, it was not the text we possess.

There is also evidence to suggest a sometimes cavalier use of the historical tradition, at least by the scribes of Uru'inimgina. Although the only episode preserved on No. 7, the invasion of Urluma, contains the essential details of that episode that we know from other compositions, it seems to be embellished with phrases that in No. 6 (Enmetena) and No. 2 (Eanatum) are attributed to other episodes. The dispatch of messengers to Urluma ("When, because of that barley,[4] he sent envoys to him;" No. 7 iv) is very close to the dispatch of messengers to Il by Enmetena ("When, because of those (boundary-) channels,[5] Enmetena . . . sent envoys to him;" No. 6 iv). In Enanatum's inscription (No. 5), the claim of Urluma to Antasura is not set into such a messenger frame. Was this frame borrowed by Uru'inimgina's scribe from the later episode concerning Il? Another possible instance of borrowing is the retreat of Urluma. A rare Sumerian word (gàr-dar) is used to describe this in No. 7, and the very same word occurs for the only other time in Old Sumerian inscriptions in the description of Il's retreat in No. 6. Finally, another rare phrase, šu-du$_7$–du$_{11}$ "to speak, act haughtily" is applied in No. 7 to Urluma; its only other occurrence is in No. 2 ii (Eanatum) to describe an early ruler of Umma whom we have identified as Ush (IV.2).

Because we have neither the original, full history of the conflict, if one ever existed, nor anything approaching all the major inscriptions dealing with it, the preceding suspicions about Uru'inimgina's composition cannot be confirmed. Just one or two additional occurrences would be enough, in this corpus, to shift a word or phrase from the "rare" to the "common" category. And there are, of course, words, phrases and topoi that persist throughout the inscriptions, regardless of episode.[6] Many are obvious from a reading of the translations and the preceding chapter. A few deserve further comment.

One is the dispatch of messengers just discussed. Diplomatic negotiation through envoys is best known from the Mari and Amarna archives centuries later than our inscriptions,[7] but the elaborate network of inter-state communication attested in those archives can now be confidently traced back to our period.[8] Umma and Lagash, being close neighbors, certainly had frequent communications, which is not to say that those reported in our inscriptions

---

[4] Sumerian *bar še-ba-ka*.

[5] Sumerian *bar e-ba-ka*.

[6] E.g. the ubiquitous construction of burial mounds for dead enemies, a practice illustrated on the Stele of the Vultures (pl. 2).

[7] See the examples of such dispatches translated in Oppenheim, *Letters from Ancient Mesopotamia* 105f., 113ff., and 119ff., and in Pritchard, *op. cit.*, 482 ff.

[8] Pettinato (Bibl. III), 95ff. We now have an actual diplomatic communication from Ebla, as Edzard is certainly correct in his reinterpretation (*Studi Eblaiti* 4,89ff.) of the text published by Pettinato, *Oriens Antiquus* 19,231ff. It is sent by Ennadagan, *en* of Mari, to the *en* of Ebla, and documents a series of conquests by earlier *en*s and *lugal*s of Mari, leading up to further conquests by Iplulil, *en* and then *lugal* of Mari, and Ennadagan, who as *en* was either a subordinate or successor of Iplulil. ("Iplulil, king [*lugal*] of Mari, defeated such-and-such, and Ennadagan, *en* of Mari made burial mounds [for them]" in section XI there, is strikingly reminiscent of our text No. 6 iii: "Enanatum, ruler of Lagash, fought with him in such-and-such. Enmetena, beloved son of Enanatum, defeated him.") Because Iplulil, known from inscriptions at Mari as king (*lugal*) of Mari (*SARI* Ma 5), is called *en* in sections V-VI of the text, but *lugal* in sections VII-XI, and occurs again as *lugal* at the text's end (section XIII), *en* at Mari may well be a vice-regent or possibly a title of an independent ruler of less prestige than *lugal*. The purpose of this unique document, which records in section VII-IX the receipt by Mari of tribute from Ebla (with Pettinato *contra* Edzard), is probably to assert territorial or hegemonistic claims of Mari over Ebla, in the same way as the messages of the rulers of Umma discussed here assert Umma's claim to parts of the Gu'edena. For a discussion of the Ebla-Mari relationship based on administrative documents, see Archi, *Studi Eblaiti* 4,129ff.

are genuine. The dispatch of messengers and communication through them is a well-known topos in Sumerian literary texts,[9] and may be used in just such a way in historical inscriptions as well: the intransigence of Umma finds literary expression in the form of a diplomatic exchange. The two such exchanges so far discussed, quoted now in full, are:

> When, because of those (boundary-) channels, Enmetena ruler of Lagash, sent envoys to Il, Il ruler of Umma, the field thief, speaking hostiley, said, "The boundary-channel of Ningirsu and the boundary-channel of Nanshe are mine! I will shift the boundary-levee from Antasura to Edimgalabzu," he said. (No. 6 iv)

> When, because of that barley, he (Enanatum I) sent envoys to him (Urluma), having them say to him, "You must deliver my barley!", Urluma spoke haughtily with him. "Antasura is mine, it is my territory!" he said. (No. 7 iv)

I have suggested above that the latter was influenced by the former, but this may not have been the case, since one additional occurrence of a messenger scene is known from a fragmentary inscription dealing with the Lagash-Umma conflict, unrelated to any episode we have yet been able to reconstruct:

> [He s]ent [envoys to . . .]: "Be it known that your city will be completely destroyed! Surrender! Be it kno[wn] that Umma will be completely destroyed! Surre[ender!"] (No. 11)

As in Sumerian literary texts, then, the messenger scene may have been a narrative device, used by the royal scribes to express the development of inter-state antagonisms. These may represent actual exchanges, or a series of exchanges, or may be a scribal fiction. We will probably never know.[10]

Another topos that recurs in our texts is that of the ruler killed by his own subjects. Such things were not uncommon in antiquity, nor are they today, but a special infamy is attached to the notion that a ruler was unsafe on his home turf, that he was so odious that his own citizens would rebel against him. It first appears in the Stela of the Vultures (No. 2 viii), where, according to my interpretation, Ningirsu, in a dream, predicts victory over Umma to Eanatum "[The people of his own city] will rise up against him (the ruler of Umma) and he will be killed within Umma itself." In No. 4, after Eanatum has re-established the border to Lagash's advantage, he invokes a curse against any leader of Umma who, in the future, crosses it. The curse ends "May there be an uprising against him in his own city!"(No. 4 iii). This is in fact what Enmetena tells us happened to the next Ummaite aggressor, Urluma. After Enmetena frustrated his attempted invasion, "Urluma escaped, but was killed in Umma itself" (No. 6 iii), and his nephew Il became ruler in his stead. Enmetena wishes a similar fate on Il or any other ruler who might violate Lagash's border: "May the people of his city, having risen up against him, kill him there within his city!" (No. 6 vi) Rebellion and assassination are invoked less literally in the curse at the end of No. 10, from Umma.

Direct divine intervention at crucial moments is sometimes a feature of historical narrative in Presargonic Lagash. By this I do not mean the divine granting of powers known from numerous royal epithets, nor am I referring to decisive actions attributed to deities but not elaborated upon, such as Enlil's drawing of the border in Nos. 3, 4 and 6;[11] defeats of enemies attributed to Ningirsu rather than an earlier ruler (Nos. 6 and 7); or the denial of

[9] See, for example, Enmerkar and the Lord of Aratta (Kramer [Bibl. I A]269ff.) or the Sumerian Sargon Legend (Cooper and Heimpel, forthcoming).

[10] The problem of the use of iconographic cliché in the historical narrative reliefs of Assyrian kings has been broached by I. Winter, "Royal Rhetoric and the Development of Historical Narrative in Neo-Assyrian Reliefs," *Studies in Visual Communication* 7,2ff.

[11] See also *SARI* La 5.2 (*ABW* Ent. 41).

Umma's claim to Lagash's territory by Enlil and Ninḥursag (IV.5). Rather, I am thinking of the lengthy episode in the Stela of the Vultures (No. 2) beginning in col. iii, where Ningirsu reacts angrily to Umma's invasion of the Gu'edena, and creates Eanatum, a superhuman hero who will avenge this violation of Ningirsu's territory. The participation of Ningirsu so directly in the events narrated ends with the long dream of Eanatum in which Ningirsu predicts his victory over Umma (vi-viii); from there on it is Eanatum's show. Although there is nothing else in our corpus to parallel Ningirsu's activity in this inscription—given the uniqueness of the Stela among surviving monuments, this is not surprising— a much smaller episode in an inscription of his brother and successor Enanatum I indicates that the Ningirsu episode in the Stela was not *sui generis*, but drew on a repertoire of motifs and phraseology present in the historical tradition of Lagash, and no doubt used in other, no longer extant, texts. The beginning of the Enanatum passage is very difficult, and it and the corresponding Stela of the Vultures passage are used to explicate one another:[12]

> Ningirsu . . . spoke angrily: "Umma has [(2 fragmentary cases)] my forage, my own property, the fields of the G[u'ede]na. (No. 2 iiif.)

> Ningirsu . . . spoke angrily: "Urluma, ruler of Umma, has said, 'Antasura is Mine!' and has marched on my very own field. He must not do violence against Enanatum, my mighty male!" (No. 5 ixf.)

The closest parallel chronologically to the elaborate participation of Ningirsu in the Stela of the Vultures is in the inscriptions of another ruler of Lagash, Gudea, several centuries later.[13] That it is Lagash again is certainly coincidence, since that state has supplied the largest body of extant royal inscriptions prior to the second millennium, thanks to the fortunate discoveries of the French excavators. Similar phenomena occur at first sporadically in the Old Babylonian period (ca. 2000-1600), as in Samsuiluna's inscription commemorating the rebuilding of the fortifications of Kish,[14] and more frequently in first millennium Assyrian and especially Babylonian inscriptions. But in the third millennium such episodes of divine activity are unusual enough to be considered, retrospectively, a kind of genre leakage: material appearing in royal inscriptions that would be more at home in either royal hymns[15] or historical-literary texts.[16]

That Lagash is the source of a large majority of third millennium inscriptions has just been mentioned. It was characterized as a coincidence because we have no reason to believe that Lagashites were more verbal than other inhabitants of Mesopotamia. It is simply that those who dug there had the luck to hit upon large numbers of historical texts from this period, whereas archaeologists and others at different sites were less fortunate. Thus, it is not easy to compare the rather rich textual material from Presargonic Lagash with contemporary inscriptions from elsewhere. But text No. 10, the only text in our dossier not in the name of a ruler of Lagash, provides some evidence that the repertoire of topoi and phraseology through which the historical traditions were expressed, was to a large extent shared with other Sumerian centers. This is to be expected from everything we have learned about Mesopotamian scribal practices and products, which, despite frequently noticeable local variation, tend to be widely disseminated without respect to state boundaries.

No. 10 tells us that when Lugalzagesi demarcated the frontier between Lagash and Umma, he

---

[12] See the notes to the full translations for details.

[13] See Kramer (Bibl. IA), 137ff.

[14] *IRSA* IVC7d.

[15] Kramer (Bibl. IA), 206; Klein, J. *Three Sulgi Hymns.*

[16] Grayson, *Babylonian Historical-Literary Texts,* and *Orientalia* 49,182ff.

constructed its (boundary-) channel, erected its monument, made its boundary-levee manifest, restored its (former) monuments. . . . He did not cross beyo[nd] its boundary-levee. He restored its (former) monuments and, at Ishtaran's command, erected a (new) monument on that spot.

These words have a familiar ring.

Eanatum . . . measured-off the boundary . . . and erected a monument on that spot. (No. 2 xf.)

Eanatum did not cross beyond the place where Mesalim had erected the monument, and (moreover) he restored that monument. (No. 3 iv)

Mesalim, king of Kish, at the command of Ishtaran, measured it off and erected a monument there. (No. 6 i)

(Eanatum) inscribed (and erected) monuments at that (boundary-) channel, and restored the monument of Mesalim, but did not cross into the plain of Umma. (No. 6 ii)

Enmetena . . . at the just command (of Enlil, Ningirsu and Nanshe) . . . constructed that (boundary-) channel. . . . He built the foundations of the (boundary-levee called) Namnundakigara. (No. 6 v)

In his curse against potential violators of his newly (re)drawn boundary, Lugalzagesi asks that

[his] city, like a place (infested) with harmful snakes, not allow him to hold his head erect! May poisonous fangs bite that ruler in his ruined palace! (No. 10 end)

In the long series of nearly identical curses against Umma in the Stela of the Vultures, the final curse, uttered in the name of the chthonic deity Ninki ("Mistress Earth"), is quite different from the others. It is not a divine battle-net that will descend from above upon Umma in punishment, as in the preceding curses, but rather,

May Ninki, by whom he has sworn, have snakes from the earth (/from below) bite Umma's feet! When Umma transgresses this (boundary-) channel, may Ninki pull the ground from under its feet! (No. 2 r. v)

Stepping outside our dossier, there are a few other non-trivial points of contact between the inscriptions from Lagash and contemporary inscriptions from other Sumerian cities. Lugalkiginedudu of Uruk (IV.5) wrote of his assumption of the title "king of Ur" (in addition to "Lord of Uruk") as follows:

When Enlil specially summoned him, and combined lordship with Kingship for him. . . . [17]

When Inana combined lordship with kingship for Lugalkiginedudu. . . . [18]

Similarly, Eanatum reports his assumption of the title King of Kish:

To Eanatum, ruler of Lagash, Inana, because she loved him so, gave him the kingship of Kish in addition to the rulership of Lagash. [19]

Enshakushana, who apparently exercised hegemony over most of Sumer for a short period of time before Lugalzagesi (IV.6), writes of his conquest of Kish and Akshak, that "he dedicated their statues, their precious metal and lapis lazuli, their timber and treasure, to Enlil at [N]ippur."[20] "Precious metals and lapis lazuli" occurs throughout No. 9 as a *per merismum* for valuables plundered, and in No. 2 r. vi, Eanatum writes that he defeated "Elam and Subartu, mountainous lands of timber and treasure." And the terms are found all together, as in Enshakushana's inscription, on the fragmentary No. 12: "Their precious

---

[17] *SARI* Uk 1.1, *IRSA* IE1c, *ABW* Lukin. v. Uruk 2.
[18] *SARI* Uk 1.2, *IRSA* IE1d, *ABW* Lukin. v. Uruk 4.
[19] *SARI* La 3.5, *IRSA* IC5b, *ABW* Ean. 2.
[20] *SARI* Uk 4.1, *IRSA* IH1b, *ABW* Ensak. v. Uruk 1.

metals and lapis lazuli, their timber and treasure, he loaded on ships."

The uses of language and interpretation of history in our earliest corpus of historical inscriptions deserve more detailed and comprehensive treatment than the tentative discussion offered here. A rigorous, synchronic literary and historical analysis of the Presargonic material should be followed by diachronic studies in which the historical inscriptions of much later times will be related back to their Early Dynastic precursors. In observing the unfolding of this genre through time, we have much to learn about ancient attitudes toward language, writing and history, and perhaps, also, something about our own.

CHAPTER VI

The Documents in Translation

The documents upon which the preceding discussion has been based are translated here, ordered and numbered as they are in Chapter II, where bibliographic and other details about the individual texts and inscribed artifacts are provided. The translations themselves are more literal than literary, in the sense that certain peculiarities of Sumerian word order and idiom are preserved. Whether this is desirable, and if so, to what extent, is controversial, and there will certainly be specialists who find these translations not literal enough (too interpretive), while others will question whether Sumerian historical texts are being well-represented in such awkward English. Were the texts here not being used as the basis for a historical reconstruction, the temptation to be more literary would not have been so firmly resisted; were the translations part of a scholarly text edition, they might have been even more literal.

The notes are intended to explicate passages that may baffle the non-specialist. More specialized notes, justifying certain readings and interpretations to my fellow Assyriologists, will appear in my *Sumerian and Akkadian Royal Inscriptions* (*SARI*). The non-specialist must be patient with the long lists of divine names, place names and temple names (beginning with E-, Sumerian for "temple") that appear in some of the inscriptions when the ruler catalogues his epithets or pious deeds. The more important gods are given in Chart 2, and important place names can be found on the maps; others are in the reference works given in the Bibliography I A-B. But a great many are minor and not really germane to the topic of this study. Brackets enclose broken text portions; pointed brackets are used to restore scribal omissions; parentheses enclose my explanatory additions.

1. URNANSHE

[i] [Urnans]he, [king of Lagash, son of Gunidu], [ii] "son" of Gursar, built the Bagar of fired bricks, and dug the Bagar.... [iii] The name of the temple is "Bagar Provides Justice." The name of the shrine is "Bagar Provides Justice."[1]

He built the Ibgal, [iv] built the temple of Nanshe, built the sanctuary of Girsu, built the Kinir, built the temple of Gatumdug, built the Tirash, built the Ningar, [v] built the temple of Ninmarki, built the Edam, built the Me-gate, built the Abzu'e, and built the wall of Lagash. He dug the Saman canal and [vi] dug the Asuhur. He fashioned (a statue of) Ninmarki, fashioned (a statue of) Nin..., fashioned (a statue of) Ningidri, fashioned (a statue of) Shulshag, fashioned (a statue of) Kindazi, [vii] fashioned (a statue of) Gushudu, fashioned (a statue of) Lama'u'e, and fashioned (a statue of) Lugalurtur.

[r.i] [Urnanshe, king] of Lagash, went to war against the leader of Ur and the leader of Umma:

The leader of Lagash [r.ii] defeated the leader of Ur. He captured Mu[...] the admiral?, [r.iii] captured Amabaragesi and Kishibgal the officer, [captured] Papursag, son of U'u, captured [...] the officer, and he made a burial mound (for them).

He defeated the leader of Umma. [r.iv] He captured Lupad and Bilala the officer, captured Pabilgaltuk ruler of Umma, captured Urgigirsag the officer, [r.v] captured Ḫursagshemaḫ the quartermaster-general, and he made a burial mound (for them).

[r.vi] The leader of Umma.[2]

Notes. [1] The translation of col. iii is very tentative. See *Revue d'Assyriologie* 74,104ff.

[2] This orphan line was either intended as a cartouche for an image of the defeated Ummaite, or is part of an unfinished sentence (see *Revue d'Assyriologie* 74,105).

2. EANATUM (Stela of the Vultures)

[i] [(20 cases broken)] He would pay it as a(n interest-bearing) [lo]an, and grain rent was imposed on it. The king of Lagash [ii] [(22 cases broken)] the leader of Umma acted haughtily? with him, and defied Lagash. Akurgal, king of Lagash, son of Urnanshe, [iii] [king of Lagash (16 cases broken)] and furthermore, he (the leader of Umma) defied Lagash regarding its (Lagash's) own property. At/regarding Pirig . . . girnunshaga, Ningirsu . . . spoke angrily: "Umma has [(2 fragmentary cases)] my forage, my own property, the fields of the [iv] G[u'ede]na."

[Lor]d? [Ni]ngirsu, [war]rior of [En]lil [(3 fragmentary cases) Ni]n[gir]su [imp]lanted the [semen] for E[a]natum in the [wom]b [(2 cases broken), and . . .] rejoiced over [Eanatum]. Inana accompanied him, named him Eana-Inana-Ibgalakakatum,[1] and set him on the special lap of Ninḫursag. Ninḫursag [offered him] her special breast. [v] Ningirsu rejoiced over Eanatum, semen implanted in the womb by Ningirsu. Ningirsu laid his span upon him, for (a length of) five forearms he set his forearm upon him: (he measured) five forearms (cubits), one span![2] Ningirsu, with great joy, [gave him] the kin[gship of Lagash].

[(1 broken and 1 frag. case)] Eanatum, who has strength, declares, "Now then, O enemy!"? For Eanatum, the name which Inana gave him, Eana-Inana-Ibgalakakatum, was [given] him as a name [(2 frag. cases)]. [Eanatum], [vi] who has strength, ordained by Ningirsu, Eanatum, [who declared?] "Now then, O enemy!", proclaimed for evermore: "The ruler of Umma—where is he recruiting?? With (other) men [. . .] he is able to exploit the Gu'edena, the beloved field of Ningirsu. May he (Ningirsu) strike him down!"

[(1 frag. and 5 broken cases)] He followed after him. Him who lies sleeping, him who lies sleeping—he approaches his head. Eanatum who lies sleeping—[his] be[loved] master [Ningirsu approaches his head. (3 cases broken)]. [vii] "Kish itself must abandon? Umma, and, being angry, cannot support it. The sun-(god) will shine at your right, and a . . . will be affixed to your forehead. O Eanatum, [(7 cases broken)] you will slay there. Their myriad corpses will reach the base of heaven. [In] Um[ma (5 cases broken) the people of his own city] [viii] will rise up against him and kill him within Umma itself. In? the . . . region you will [. . . . " (18 cases broken)].

[ix] He fought with him. A person shot an arrow at Eanatum. He was shot through? by the arrow and had difficulty moving. He cried out in the face of it. The person . . . [(12 cases broken or frag.)]. [x] Eanatum provoked a windstorm in Umma, unleashed? a deluge there [(7 cases broken)]. Eanatum, the man of just commands, [xi] measured off the boundary [with the leader of Umma?], left (some land) under Umma's control, and erected a monument on that spot. The leader of Umma [(6 cases broken). He defeated Umma?] and made twenty b[urial mounds] for it. Eanatum, over whom Shulutul cries sweet tears, [Eanatum] . . . ; E[anatum . . .] destroyed the foreign lands; [Eanatum] restored to [xii] Ningirsu's control [his] belov[ed fi]eld, the Gu'eden[a. (6 cases broken)]. The field Dana in the Kiḫara of Ningirsu, he [(5 cases broken). Ea]natum [xiii] erected a [monument] in the grand temple of [Ningirsu.[3] (10 cases broken or frag.)] [of Ningirsu], Ean[atum is the . . .] of Ningirsu. His personal god < is Shulutul>. [xiv] The fields Badag [(49 cases broken or frag.)[4] Eanatum, nomi]nated by [Ni]ngirsu, restored to his (Ningirsu's) [control].

Eanatum gave the great battle net of Enlil to the leader of Umma, and made him swear to him by it. The leader of Umma swore to Eanatum: "By the life of Enlil, king of heaven and earth! I may exploit the field of Ningirsu as a(n interest-bearing) loan. I shall not . . . the irrigation channel! F[orever and evermore, I shall not transgress the territory of Ningirsu! I shall not shift (the course of) its irrigation channels and canals! I shall not smash its monuments! Whenever I do transgress, may the great battle net of Enlil, king of heaven and earth?, by which I have sworn, descend upon Umma!" Eanatum was very clever indeed! He made up the eyes of two doves with kohl, and adorned their heads with cedar (foliage). xviiHe released them to Enlil, king of heaven and earth,? to the Ekur? in Nippur: "After what he has declare]d and has reiterated [to my master Enlil], if any leader in Umma reneges against the agreement, when he opposes or contests the agreement, whenever he violates this agreement, may the great battle net of Enlil, by which he has sworn, descend upon Umma!"

Eanatum gave the great battle net of Ninhursag to the leader of Umma, and made him swear to him by it. The leader of Umma swore to Eanatum: ["By the life of Ninhursag! I may exploit the field of Ningirsu as a(n interest-bearing) loan. I shall not . . . the irrigation channel! Forever and evermore, I shall not transgress the territory of Ningirsu! I shall not shift (the course of) its irrigation channels and canals! I shall not smash its monuments! Whenever I do transgress, may the great battle net of Ninhursag, by which I have sworn, descend upon Umma!" Eanatum] xviiiwas very clever indeed! He made up the eyes of two doves with kohl, and adorned their heads with cedar (foliage). He r[eleased them] to Ninhursag in Kesh: "After what he has declared and has reiterated to [my] mother Ninhursag, if any leader [in] Umma re[neg]es, when [he opposes or contests the agree]-ment, [wh]enever [he violates this agreement], may the great [battle net] of Ninhursag, by which he has sworn, descend upon Umma!"

Eanatum [gave the great battle net of Enki, king of Abzu, to the leader of Umma, and made him swear by it: "By the life of Enki, king of Abzu! I may exploit the field of Ningirsu as a(n interest-bearing) loan. I shall not . . . the irrigation channel! Forever and evermore, I shall not transgress the territory of Ningirsu! I shall not shift (the course of) its irrigation channels and canals! I shall not smash its monuments!] xixWhenever I do transgress, may the great battle net of Enki, king of Abzu, descend upon Umma!" Ea[natum was very clever indeed! He made up the eyes of two doves with kohl, and adorned their heads with cedar (foliage).] He released them [to Enki? in the . . .] of Ningirsu. Eanatum swore? by the carp set? toward the Abzu: "After what he has declared [and has reiterated] to my master Enki, [if any leader in Umma reneges, when he opposes or contests the agreement, whenever he violates this agreement, may the great battle net of Enki, by which he has sworn, descend upon Umma!"

Eanatum] gave [the great battle net] xxof Sin, the impetuous calf of Enlil, to the leader of Umma, and made him swear to him by it. The leader of Umma swore [to Eanatum: "By the life of Sin, the impetuous calf of Enlil!] I may exploit [the field of Ningirsu as a(n interest-bearing) loan.] I will not . . . the irrigation channel! Forever and evermore, I shall not transgress the territory of Ningirsu! xxiI shall not shift (the course of) its irrigation channels and canals! I shall not smash its monuments! Whenever I do transgress, may the great battle net of Sin, impetuous calf [of Enlil, by which I have sworn,] descend [upon Umma]!" Eanatum was very clever indeed! He made up the eyes of four doves with kohl, and adorned their heads with cedar (foliage). [He released] two of them towards xxii[the Ekishnugal?] in Ur, [and he released two toward . . . , the holy?] dwel[ling] of Sin: "After what he has declared and has reiterated [to my master? Sin,] impetuous calf of Enlil, if any leader in Umma reneges, when he opposes or [contests the agreement,? whenever he violates this agreement, may the great battle net of Sin, impetuous calf of Enlil, by which he has sworn, descend upon Umma!"]

r.iEanatum gave the great battle net of Utu, king of . . . , to the leader of Umma, and made him swear to him by it. The leader of Umma swore to Eanatum: "By the life of Utu, [king of . . . ! I may exploit the field of Ningirsu as a(n interest-bearing) loan. I will not . . . the irrigation channel! Forever and eveomore,] I shall not transgress the territory of Ningirsu! I shall not shift (the course of) its irrigation channels and canals! I shall not smash its monuments! Whenever I do transgress, may the great battle net of Utu, king of . . . , by which I have sworn, descend upon Umma!" Eanatum was very clever indeed! He made up the eyes of two doves with kohl, and adorned their heads with cedar (foliage). For Utu, king of . . . , in the Ebabbar at Larsa, he had them offered as sacrificial bulls?: r.ii"After that which he has declared and reiterated to my m[aster Utu], if any leader in U[mma] reneges, when he opposes or contests the agreement, whenever he violates this agreement, may the great battle net of Utu, king of . . . , by which he has sworn, r.iii[descend upon] Umma!"

[Eanatum . . . to the leader of Umm]a[. . . ,] and made him thereby invoke the name of Ninki. The leader of Umma swore to Eanatum: "By the life of Ninki! r.ivI may exploit [the field of Ningirsu] as a(n interest-bearing) loan. I will not . . . the irrigation channel! Forever and evermore, r.v[I shall not transgress] the territory [of Ningirsu!] I shall not shift (the course of) its irrigation channels and canals! I shall not [smash] its monuments! Whenever I do transgress, may Ninki, [whose] name I have [invoked], have sn[akes from the ground] bite Umma's feet! When Umma [transgresses] this [(boundary-) channel may Ninki pull the ground out from under its feet!" Eanatum was very clever indeed?. (3 cases broken) "After that which he has declared and reiterated to Ninki . . . , if any leader in Umma rene]ges, when he opposes or contests the agreement, whenever he violates this agreement, may Ninki, by whom he has sworn, have snakes from the ground bite Umma's feet!⁵ When Umma transgresses this (boundary-) channel, may Ninki pull the ground out from under its feet!"

Eanatum, king of Lagash, granted strength by Enlil, nourished with special milk by Ninhursag, given a fine name by Inana, granted wisdom by Enki, chosen in her heart by Nanshe the mighty queen, who subj[ugates foreign lands for] r.viN[ingirsu], beloved of [Dumuzi'abzu], nominated by Hendursaga, beloved friend of Lugalurub, beloved spouse of Inana; [defeate]d Elam and Subartu, mountainous lands of timber and [treasure,] r.vii[(x cases broken) he] de[feated . . .], defeated Susa, [defeated] the ruler of Urua, who stood with the (city's) emblem in the vanguard,? r.viii[(x cases broken)] and destroyed Arua. . . . Sumer r.ix[(x cases broken)]. He defeated U[r r.x(14 cases broken).

Eanatum (2 cases broken)], who restored the Gu'edena to (Ningirsu's) [con]trol, Eanatum r.xi[(19 cases broken)] of N[ingirsu], who erected (this monument) for Ningirsu—the name of the monument—it is not a man's (name)?—he proclaimed its name: "Ningirsu, the lord, crown of Luma is the life of the Pirigedena-canal!" He [erected for him (Ningirsu)] the monument of the Gu'edena, the beloved field of Ningirsu, which Eanatum restored to Ningirsu's control.

Legends next to figures of Eanatum in the upper and middle registers, rev.:
Eanatum, who subjugates foreign lands for Ningirsu.

Legend next to an enemy in the lower register, rev.:
Al[. . .], king of Kish.⁶

Notes. ¹ The full name of Eanatum, meaning "Worthy in the (temple) Eana of Inana of Ibgal."
² Sumerian *kùš* means both "forearm" and "cubit" (as English "cubit" is from the Latin for "forearm"). A cubit is ca. 50 cm.; a span is 1/2 cubit. Eanatum's height then, is 2.75 m. or 9'2"!

[3] Refering to this stela.

[4] At least twenty field names were listed. They are mostly broken, or preserve only the word "field" and traces of the name.

[5] The puns involved here do not come across in translation. Ninki (Mistress Earth) is a chthonic deity, and whereas the battle-nets of the gods in the previous oaths and curses are said to descend (lit. "fall from above, heaven") upon Umma, the snakes here are coming up "from the earth" (*ki-ta*), which also means "from below."

[6] Jacobsen (Bibl. III), 387 n. 77 and 393 n. 90 thinks this name is that of Kalbum, a king of Kish known from the Sumerian King List. For the unlikelihood of this suggestion, see *SARI* ad loc.

3. EANATUM (Boulders)

[i] [After? E]nlil demarcated [the boundary between Ningirsu and Shara], and Mesalim erected a monument there, and at his orders [(3 cases broken)].

[ii] [(3 cases broken) the leader of Umma] smashed that monument, and marched on the plain of Lagash. The field Usarda'u, the field Sumbubu, the field Eluḫa, the field Kimari, the field Du'ashri,[1] [(4 cases frag.) [iii] (4 cases frag.)] of [N]ingir[su . . .]. These the leader of Umma invaded,? and smashed the monument. He named it "The leader of Umma . . . the field;" he named it[2] "The leader of Umma marched there;" [iv] he named it "The leader of Umma added there."

Eanatum, ruler of Lagash, granted strength by Enlil, nourished with special milk by Nin-ḫursag, given a fine name by Nanshe, who subjugates foreign lands for Ningirsu, restored to Ningirsu's control his beloved fields. Eanatum did not cross beyond the place where Mesalim had erected the monument, and (moreover) he restored that monument.

Notes: [1] The break contains possibly eight additional field names.
          [2] "It" is either the fields, or a new monument erected by the Ummaite leader.

4. EANATUM[1] (Clay Vase)

[i] [Enli]l, [by his authoritative command, demarcated the boundary between] N[ingirs]u [an]d [Shara. Mesalim, king of Kish, at the command of Ishtaran, measured it off and erected a monument there].?[2] *The leader of Umma smashed that [monume]nt and march-ed on the plain of Lagash.* [ii] [Ningirsu] gave the order to Eanatum, and he destroyed Umma. At the [pla]ce where Mesalim had erected a monument, [E]an[at]um, [at Ningirsu's command], [*establish*]ed a mo[*nument*]. *When he thereby established the monument,* [iii] [Eanatu]m [n]amed it "*Ningirsu is the lord eternally exalted in Abzu.*"

If [a leader of] Um[ma] [iii] [cros]ses the water/canal in order to take away the fields, may Ningirsu be a (hostile) dragon to him! May Enlil make salt surface in his furrows! [May] Shu . . . [. . . !] *May . . . not give hi[m] life! May he not . . . !* [May . . . not] give him [. . . !] May there be an uprising against him in his own city!

Notes: [1] The inscription is restored from two sets of fragments; it has not been conclusively proved that they belong together, although many factors suggest they do. Italics are used here to separate the two sets.
          [2] Restored after No. 6 i; alternatively, restore after the damaged No. 3.

5. ENANATUM I

[i]For Hendursaga, chief herald of Abzu, Enanatum, [ru]ler of [Laga]sh, [granted strength?] by Enlil, nourished with special milk by Ninhursag, chosen in her heart by Nanshe, [ii]chief executive for Ningirsu, specially summoned by Inana, nominated by Hendursaga, son begotten by Lugalurub, son of Akurgal ruler of Lagash, [iii]beloved brother of Eanatum, ruler of Lagash—

When he built the Ibgal for Inana, made the Eana surpassing in all lands, and [iv]decorated it for her with gold and silver; (when) he built his "palace" of the Sacred Precinct for Hendursaga, and decorated it for him with gold and silver; (when) he restored his temple for Nindar; (when) he built [v]their *giguna* for Nin[girsu and Ba'u?]; (when) he built his "palace" of Urub for Lugalurub, and decorated it for him with gold and silver; (when) [vi]he built [her Esagug] for Amageshtinana, built a w[ell] of fired brick for her, and set up? . . . ;(when) he [built] the Eshd[ugru for Ningirsu; (then) he (3 cases broken)].

[vii][When Enlil?] turned over control of Umma to [Nin]g[ir]s[u], and he then put it in Enanatum's control, Urluma, ruler of Umma, [viii][recruited foreigners] and transgressed the boundary-channel of Ningirsu. "Antasura is mine! I shall exploit (its) produce?!" he said, and [ix]he awaited him at Du'urgiga.

Ningirsu spoke angrily: "Urluma, ruler of Umma, has said, 'Antasura is mine!' and [x]has marched on my very own field. He must not do violence against Enanatum, my mighty male!"

Enanatum beat back Urluma, ruler of Umma, to the boundary-channel [xi]of Ningirsu. He went after him at the . . . of the Lumagirnunta (-canal), and . . . his . . . garment.[1]

Enanatum, who built the temple of Hendursaga—his personal god is Shulutul.[2]

[xii](blank)

[xiii]He (Enanatum) had it inscribed on the copper standard and the . . . of the copper standard fixed on (a pole? of) wood belonging to Hendursaga.[3] [Sh]ul[ut]ul, the [loy]al [personal god] of [En]metena has checked it.? He (Hendursaga?) is the owner [of the standard].

Notes: [1] An obscure Sumerian idiom here having to do with an outer garment, provides an ambiguous ending for the battle report.

   [2] The actual inscription ends here, separated by the blank col. xii from the notation that follows.

   [3] One imagines, perhaps, a figure of Shulutul holding a pole with a metal standard, similar to the poles with standards that developed out of the earlier ring bundel, held by "hero" figures in Sargonic glyptic. Such a standard, made entirely of copper, was actually excavated at Girsu (de Sarzec, *Découvertes en Chaldée*, pl. 57/1; but cf. Seidl, *RLA* 6,317b).

6. ENMETENA

[i]Enlil, king of all lands, father of all the gods, by his authoritative command, demarcated the border between Ningirsu and Shara.[1] Mesalim, king of Kish, at the command of Ishtaran,[2] measured it off and erected a monument there.

Ush, ruler of Umma, acted arrogantly: he smashed that monument and marched on the plain of Lagash. Ningirsu, warrior of Enlil, at his (Enlil's) just command, did battle with Umma. At Enlil's command, he cast the great battle-net upon it, and set up burial mounds for it on the plain.

Eanatum, ruler of Lagash, uncle of Enmetena ruler of Lagash, demarcated the border with Enakale, ruler of Umma. [ii]He extended the (boundary-) channel from the Nun-canal to the Gu'edena, leaving (a) 215-*nindan* (1290 m.) (strip) of Ningirsu's land under Umma's control and establishing a no-man's land there. He inscribed (and erected) monuments at that (boundary-) channel and restored the monument of Mesalim, but did not cross into the plain of Umma. On the boundary-levee of Ningirsu, (called) Namnundakigara, he built a chapel of Enlil, a chapel of Ninḫursag, a chapel of Ningirsu and a chapel of Utu.

The leader of Umma could exploit one *guru* (5184 hl.) of the barley of Nanshe and the barley of Ningirsu as a(n interest-bearing) loan. It bore interest, and 8,640,000 *guru* (44,789,760,000 hl.) accrued.[3] Since he was unable to repay? that barley, Urluma, ruler of Umma, diverted water into the boundary-channel of Ningirsu and the boundary-channel of Nanshe. He set fire to their monuments and smashed them, and destroyed the established chapels of the gods that were built on the (boundary-levee called) Namnundakigara. [iii]He recruited foreigners, and transgressed the boundary-channel of Ningirsu. Enanatum, ruler of Lagash, fought with him in the Ugiga-field, the field of Ningirsu. Enmetena, beloved son of Enanatum, defeated him. Urluma escaped, but was killed in Umma itself. He had abandoned sixty teams of asses at the bank of the Lumagirnunta-canal, and left the bones of their personnel strewn over the plain. He (Enmetena) made burial mounds in five places there for them.

At that time, Il, who was the temple-estate administrator at Zabala, had marched in retreat from Girsu to Umma. Il took the rulership of Umma for himself. He diverted water into the boundary-channel of [iv]Ningirsu and the boundary-channel of Nanshe, at the boundary-levee of Ningirsu in the direction of the bank of the Tigris in the region of Gir-su,[4] the Namnundakigara of Enlil, Enki and Ninḫursag. He repaid? (only) 3600 *guru* (18,662,400 hl.) of Lagash's barley.

When, because of those (boundary-) channels, Enmetena ruler of Lagash, sent envoys to Il, Il ruler of Umma, the field thief, speaking hostiley, said: "The boundary-channel of Ningirsu and the boundary-channel of Nanshe are mine! I will shift the boundary-levee from Antasura to Edimgalabzu," he said. But Enlil and Ninḫursag did not allow him (to do) this.

[v]Enmetena, ruler of Lagash, nominee of Ningirsu, at the just command of Enlil, at the just command of Ningirsu, and at the just command of Nanshe, constructed that (boundary-) channel from the Tigris to the Nun-canal. He built the foundations of the (levee called) Namnundakigara for him (Ningirsu) out of stone, restoring it for the master who loves him, Ningirsu, and for the mistress who loves him, Nanshe.

Enmetena, ruler of Lagash, granted the scepter by Enlil, granted wisdom by Enki, chosen in Nanshe's heart, chief executive for Ningirsu, who carries out the commands of the gods— [vi]may his personal god, Shulutul, forever stand (interceding) before Ningirsu and Nanshe for the life of Enmetena!

If the leader of Umma transgresses the boundary-channel of Ningirsu and the boundary-channel of Nanshe, to take away fields by force—whether he be the leader of Umma or an(y) other leader—may Enlil destroy him! May Ningirsu, after casting his great battle-net upon him, bring down upon him his giant hands and feet! May the people of his city, having risen up against him, kill him there within his city!

Notes: [1] That is, between Lagash, whose god was Ningirsu, and Umma, whose god was Shara.
[2] The god Ishtaran is also responsible for the border in the inscription of Lugalzagesi, No. 10.
[3] See the discussion in IV.4.
[4] This probably refers to a western branch of the Tigris, near Girsu. See III.1.

7. URU'INIMGINA (Clay Disk)

[i] [(ca. 15 cases broken)] ... silver, if he bought sheep, someone would take away the high quality sheep among those sheep.

The *guda*-priests paid grain taxes at Ambar, and those *guda*-priests had to build a (store?) house at Ambar for those grain taxes.

When the [(2 cases broken)], foremen, lamentation singers, agricultural supervisors or brewers brought a wool-sheep and had it sheared at the palace, if the sheep was white, the wool was taken by the palace and they also had to pay five shekels of silver.

The oxen of the gods plowed the garlic [plot] of the [r]uler, and [the bes]t [fields of the gods became the garlic and cucumber plots of the ruler. (ca. 15 cases broken)].

[ii] [(ca. 15 cases broken)] the *iginudu* was also appropriated for (work on) [the irrigation channels?] which were [in the field], and the *shublugal*, as long as he (the *iginudu*) was doing his work,? did not allow him to drink water. He was not even allowed to drink water as an ass (would be)!

If a poor person made a fish-pond?, someone would make off with the fish in it, and that (poor) man would (only be able to) say "Oh Sungod!"[1]

If a man divorced his wife, the ruler took five shekels of silver and the chancellor took one shekel of silver. If a man smeared kohl on the head (of someone else),[2] the ruler took five shekels of silver, the chancellor took one shekel of silver, and the sage took one shekel of silver. [If?] a man ... [(ca. 15 cases broken)].

[iii] [(ca. 15 cases broken)] the ruler, the chancellor and the sage no longer take silver.

If a poor man makes a fish pond,? no one makes off with its fish. He (Uru'inimgina) abolished the crime of theft. Lost items are (now) displayed at the city-gate.

If a woman speaks ... disrespectfully? to a man, that woman's mouth is crushed with a fired brick, and the fired brick is displayed at the city-gate. Women of former times each married two men,[3] but women of today have been made to give up that crime.

The dream-interpreter, the seer, the ..., and the carpenter at the building site? ... [(ca. 15 cases broken)].

[iv] [(ca. 15 cases broken)] When, because of that barley, he (Enanatum I) sent envoys to him (Urluma), having them say to him, "You must deliver my barley!", Urluma spoke haughtily with him. "Antasura is mine, it is my territory!" he said. He levied the Ummaites, and foreigners were dispatched? there. At the Ugiga-field, the beloved field of Ningirsu, Ningirsu destroyed the Ummaite levies. He confronted the retreating Urluma, ruler of Umma, at the base of the Lumagirnunta-canal, and he (Urluma) abandoned his sixty teams of asses there, and left the bones of their per[sonnel strewn over the plan. (ca. 12 cases broken)].

[v] [(ca. 12 cases broken) (for Ningirsu)] he built [...]; he built the brewery which provides great vats? of wine for its master; and he dug his beloved canal, the Pasamanukashdu. He built the temple of Ba'u. For Igalim, he built the Emehushgalanki; for Shulshagana he built his Kitushakkil. For Hegir, beloved *lukur*-priestess of Ningirsu, he built her temple; for Lamashaga, his guide,? he built her temple; [for] Ninsar, Nin[girsu's] butcher, [he built his temple. (ca 10 cases broken)].

Notes: [1] The sungod Utu was the god of Justice, to whom the victim of a crime cried out. The implication here is that the victim lacked more concrete recourse. The phrase "Oh Sungod!" became a synonym of "crime" or "oppression."
   [2] Possibly a gesture in a betrothal or marriage rite.
   [3] The statement is unambiguous, but must be understood as hyperbole, as must many of the other representations of "former times." For other interpretations (fratriarchal family structure; avoidance of high divorce fees), see the commentary in *ABW*.

8. URU'INIMGINA (Cylinder Fragment)

^{i'}[(x cases broken) For Nanshe,] he built [her beloved canal], the Ni[na]dua-canal, built the Eninnu at its beginning and buil[t] the Esirara at its [en]d. [(x cases broken)]

^{ii'}[(x cases broken)] After rejoicing over it,? on the tenth day they were very happy. "What (fault) do I have?" he said to him. "I have committed no violence." Uruda? ... [(x cases broken)]

^{iii'}[(x cases broken)] He besieged? Girsu. Uru'inimgina battled him and . . . its (Girsu's) wall. . . . He returned to his city, but [he] came a second time [(x cases broken)].

9. URU'INIMGINA (Clay Tablet)

ⁱThe leader of Umma set fire to the Eki⌐bira¬. He set fire to the Antasura and bundled off its precious metals and lapis-lazuli. He plundered? the "palace" of Tirash, he plundered? the Abzubanda, he plundered? the chapels of Enlil and Utu. ⁱⁱHe plundered? the Aḫush and bundled off its precious metals and lapis-lazuli; he plundered? the Ebabbar and bundled off its precious metals and lapis-lazuli; he plundered? the *giguna* of Ninmaḫ in the sacred grove ⁱⁱⁱand bundled off its precious metals and lapis-lazuli; he plundered? the Bagar and bundled off its precious metals and lapis-lazuli; he set fire to the Dugru and bundled off its precious metals and lapis-lazuli; he plundered? the Abzu-ega; he set fire to the temple of Gatumdug, ^{iv}bundled off its precious metals and lapis-lazuli, and destroyed its statuary; he set fire to the shrine Eana of Inana, bundled off its precious metals and lapis-lazuli and destroyed its statuary; he plundered? the Shapada and bundled off its precious metals and lapis-lazuli.

^vIn Ḫenda, he overturned. . . . In Ki'es, he plundered? the temple of Nindar and bundled off its precious metals and lapis-lazuli; in Kinunir he set fire to the temple of Dumuzi-abzu and bundled off its precious metals and lapis-lazuli; he set fire to the temple of Lugalurub and ^{vi}bundled off its precious metals and lapis-lazuli; he plundered? Nanshe's E'engura and bundled off its precious metals and lapis-lazuli; in Sag[ug] ^{vii}he plundered? the temple of Amageshtinana, bundled off its precious metals and lapis-lazuli and threw them in a well.?

In the fields of Ningirsu, whichever were cultivated, he destroyed the barley.

The leader of Umma, hav[ing] sacked L[ag]ash, has committed a sin against Ningirsu. The hand which he has raised against him will be cut off! It is not a sin of Uru'inimgina, king of Girsu! May Nisaba, the goddess of Lugalzagesi, ruler of Umma, make him (Lugalzagesi) bear the sin!

10. LUGALZAGESI

[(ca. 8-10 cases broken) b]orn for . . . , fierce-headed noble of Sumer, irresistible in all the lands, *en*-priest intimate? with Ninur, ¹⁰ . . . counselled by Enki, beloved friend of Ishtaran, mighty executive for Enlil, king nominated by Inana, constructed its (boundary-) ditch, erected its monument, made its boundary-mound manifest, ²⁰restored its (former) monuments, [(2 cases broken)].

This is the frontier according to the monument of Shara: fr[om] the Al . . . -canal [to] the Dua-canal is 45 *nind*[*an*] (27 km.).

This is the frontier according to the monum[ent of] Shara: [from the Dua]-cana[l ³⁰to . . . is x *nindan*.

This is the frontier according to the monument of Shara: from . . . to Ḫaral is x *nindan*].

This is the frontier according to the monumen[t of Shara;] fr[om] Ḥaral [to] the fortress . . . ra [40] is 21,630 nind[an] (129.78 km.).[1]

This is the frontier according to the monument of Shara: from the fortress . . . ra to Nagnanshe is 636[2] *nindan* (3.816 km.).

This is the frontier according to the monument of Shara: from the Nagnanshe to the Gibil-canal is 1180 *nindan* (7.08 km.).

[50] This is the frontier according to the monument of Shara: from the Gibil-canal to Edimgalabzu is 960 *ninda[n]* (5.76 km.).

[This is the] f[rontier according to 'the monument of Shara] : from E[di]mgalabz[u] to Murgushara is 790 *nindan* (4.74 km.).

This is the [f]rontier according to the monument of Shara: from [Mur]gu<shara> [60] to [. . .]ishtaran is [. . .] *nindan*.

This is [the frontier] according to [the mo]nument of Shara: [f]rom [. . .]ishtaran to [Anza]gar is [12]80[?] *nindan* (7.68 km.).

This is [the frontier] according to [the m]onument of Shara: from [Anza]gar [to . . . is . . . *nindan*].

[70] [(x cases broken)] He did not go beyo[nd] its boundary-levee. He restored its (former) monuments and, at Ishtaran's command,[3] [80] erected a (new) monument on that spot.

If another leader[4] destroys[?] it there, or takes it away and makes off (with it), may [his] city, like a place (infested) with harmful snakes, not allow him to hold his head erect.[5] [90] May poisonous fangs bite that ruler in his ruined palace!

Notes: [1] Probably to be emended to 390 *nindan* (ca. 2.34 km.).
[2] Or 63'7'. The stone tablet seems to have 617, which could be an error for 637.
[3] See n. 2 to No. 6.
[4] Literally "man;" see chap. I.
[5] There is a pun here on the Sumerian *sag-íl* "to hold the head erect," which usually means to have pride and self-confidence, but here is also to be understood literally within the terms of the metaphor: in order to watch out for the poisonous snakes on the ground, the ruler must keep his head directed downward. Cf. the curse in No. 2 rev. v, and chap. V.

11. RULER'S NAME NOT PRESERVED (Clay Vessel Fragment)

[(x columns missing) i'(traces only) ii'(x cases missing) " . . .] my field. . . . " Enlil [(x cases broken).

iii'(x cases broken)] which had escaped, in Umma, Ningirsu. . . . Nanshe [(x cases broken).

iv'(x cases broken) He s]ent [envoys to . . .]: "Be it known that your city will be completely destroyed! Surrender! Be it kno[wn] that Umma will be completely destroyed! Surre[nder!" (x cases missing) v'(traces only) (x columns missing)].

12. RULER'S NAME NOT PRESERVED (Clay Vessel Fragment)

[(x columns missing?) i'(traces) ii'(x cases broken)] he bound the arms of [the per]-so[n]nel abandoned there. Their precious metal and lapis-lazuli, their timber and treasure, he loaded on ships.

A tenth time, Lugal . . . ,[1] ruler of Uruk, dispatched troops. "Bitter" grain, . . . [grain], . . . grain [(x cases broken)].

iii'[(x cases broken) he]. . . . [2]

Notes: [1] Written *lugal-TAR*.

 [2] The verb ending the inscription can mean "offer, load, bear;" note the end of No. 9 with the same verb. But here it is tempting to restore this fragment with another fragment found with it (*ABW* An Lag 10), to yield the following conclusion to the inscription: "He (the ruler of Lagash) cultivated the fields of the Gu'edena for him (Ningirsu), and offered to him its [grain] (in the amount of) [x] *guru*." The mention of the Gu'edena would put these hostilities with Uruk in the context of the continuing struggle between Lagash and Umma, supporting the notion of close cooperation between Umma and southern Sumer against Lagash. Is *Lugal-TAR* of Uruk here an ally of Lugalzagesi, before the latter took the title "king of Uruk," or does this text narrate earlier events in the Lagash-Umma dispute?

BIBLIOGRAPHY

I. Mesopotamian History and Civilization

A. GENERAL WORKS

    Adams, R. Mc., *Heartland of Cities*, 1981.

    Bottéro, J., *The Near East: The Early Civilizations*, 1965.

    Cambridge Ancient History (3rd ed.), vols. I/1-2 (*CAH*), 1970.

    Kramer, S. N., *The Sumerians*, 1963.

    Oppenheim, A. L., *Ancient Mesopotamia*, 1964.

    Reallexikon der Assyriologie (*RLA*), 1928-.

    Redman, C., *The Rise of Civilization*, 1978.

B. NAMES OF GODS, PLACES, AND TEMPLES (in addition to the works listed above)

    Edzard, D. O., "Mesopotamien" in H. Haussig, *Wörterbuch der Mythologie I*, 1963.

    Edzard, D. O., G. Farber, and E. Sollberger, *Répertoire géographique des textes cunéiformes I*, (*RGTC*), 1974.

    Falkenstein, A., *Die Inschriften Gudeas von Lagaš I* (Analecta Orientalia 30), 1966.

C. CHRONOLOGY

    Boese, J., *Altmesopotamische Weihplatten*, chap. 3, 1971.

    Braun-Holzinger, E., *Frühdynatische Beterstatuetten*, 1977.

    Huber, Peter J. et. al., *Astronomical Dating of Babylon I and Ur III*, 1982.

    Jacobsen T., *The Sumerian King List* (Assyriological Studies 11), 1939.

    Nagel, W., "Frühdynastische Epochen in Mesopotamien," *Vorderasiatische Archäologie. Studien... Anton Moortgat... gewidmet*, 178ff., 1964.

    Nagel, W., "Zur Datierung der Frühsumerischen Kultur," *Berliner Jahrbuch für Vor-und Frühgeschichte* 8, 120ff., 1968.

    Nissen, H., *Zur Datierung des Königsfriedhofs von Ur*, part 2, 1966.

    Porada, E. and D. Hansen, "The Relative Chronology of Mesopotamia" in R. Ehrich, *Old World Chronologies*, 133ff., 1965.

    Rowton, M., "Chronology. Ancient Western Asia," *CAH* 1/1 Chap. VI/2, 1970.

D. ART

    Moortgat, A., *The Art of Ancient Mesopotamia*, 1969.

    Parrot, A., *Sumer*, 1960.

    Strommenger, E., *5000 Years of the Art of Mesopotamia*, 1964.

II. The Lagash-Umma Conflict

Jacobsen, T., "A Survey of the Girsu (Tello) Region," *Sumer* 25, 103ff., 1969.

Lambert, M., "La guerre entre Urukagina et Lugalzagesi," *Rivista degli Studi Orientali* 50, 29ff., 1976.

Lambert, M., "L'occupation du Girsu par Urlumma roi d'Umma," *Revue d'Assyriologie* 59, 81ff., 1965.

Lambert, M., "Le quartier Lagash," *Rivista degli Studi Orientali* 32, 123ff., 1957.

Lambert, M., "Une histoire du conflit entre Lagash et Umma," *Revue d'Assyriologie* 59, 141ff., 1965

Pettinato, G., "Il conflitto tra Lagas ed Umma per la 'Frontiera Divina' et la sua soluzione . . . ," *Mesopotamia* 5/6.281ff., 1970-71.

Poebel, A., "Der Konflikt zwischen Lagas und Umma zur Zeit Enannatums I. und Entemenas," *Paul Haupt Anniversary Volume.* 220ff., 1926.

Sollberger, E., "Urukagina, roi de Girsu," *Proceedings* of the 22nd International Congress of Orientalists, 29ff., 1953.

Westenholz, A., "Diplomatic and Commercial Aspects of Temple Offerings . . . ," *Iraq* 39, 19ff., 1977.

III. Other Works on Presargonic Babylonia

Bauer, J., *Altsumerische Wirtschaftsurkunden aus Lagasch*, 1967.

Charvát, P., "The Growth of Lugalzagesi's Empire," *Festschrift L. Matouš*, 43ff., 1978.

Diakonoff, I. M., *Structure of Society and State in Early Dynastic Sumer*, 1974.

Edzard, D., "'Soziale Reformen' in Zweistromland," in J. Harmatta and G. Komoróczy, *Wirtschaft und Gesellschaft im alten Vorderasien*, 145ff., 1976.

Fiandra, E., "Attività a Kish di un mercante di Lagash," *Oriens Antiquus* 20, 165ff., 1981.

Foster, B., "A New Look at the Sumerian Temple State," *Journal of the Economic and Social History of the Orient* 24, 225ff., 1981.

Gelb, I., "Ebla and the Kish Civilization," in L. Cagni, *La Lingua di Ebla*, 9ff., 1981.

Grégoire, J. P., *La province méridionale de l'état de Lagash*.

Hallo, W., *Early Mesopotamian Royal Titles*, 1957.

Hruška, B., "Die Reformtexte Urukaginas," *Compte rendue*, Rencontre Assyriologique Internationale 19, 151ff., 1972.

Jacobsen, T., "Early Political Development in Mesopotamia," in *Toward the Image of Tammuz*, 132ff., 1970.

Lambert, M., "L'expansion de Lagash au temps d'Entemena," *Rivista degli Studi Orientali* 47, 1ff., 1972.

Lambert, M., "Ur-Emush 'grand-marchand' de Lagash," *Oriens Antiquus* 20, 176ff., 1981.

Maekawa, K., "The Development of the E-MI in Lagash During Early Dynastic III," *Mesopotamia* 8/9, 77ff., 1973-74.

Nissen, H., "Short Remarks on Early State-Formation in Babylonia," in M. Larsen, *Power and Propaganda*, 145ff., 1979.

Pettinato, G., *The Archives of Ebla*, 1981.

Powell, M., "Texts from the Time of Lugalzagesi. Problems and Perspectives in Their Interpretation," *Hebrew Union College Annual* 49, 1ff., 1978.

Rosengarten, Y., *Le concept sumérien de consommation dans la vie économique et religieuse*, 1961.

Sollberger, E., "L'opposition au pays de Sumer et Akkad," in A. Finet, *La voix de l'opposition*, 1973.

Vanstiphout, H., "Political Ideology in Early Sumer," *Orientalia Lovaniensia Periodica*, 7ff., 1970.

Westenholz, A., "The Old Akkadian Empire in Contemporary Opinion," in M. Larsen, *Power and Propaganda*, 107ff., 1979.

IV. Translations of Royal Inscriptions

Cooper, J. S., *Sumerian and Akkadian Royal Inscriptions (SARI)*. 1 (forthcoming)

Sollberger, E. and J. R. Kupper, *Inscriptions royales sumériennes et akkadiennes (IRSA)*, 1971.

Steible, H. and H. Behrens, *Die altsumerische Bau-und Weihinschriften (ABW)*, 1982.

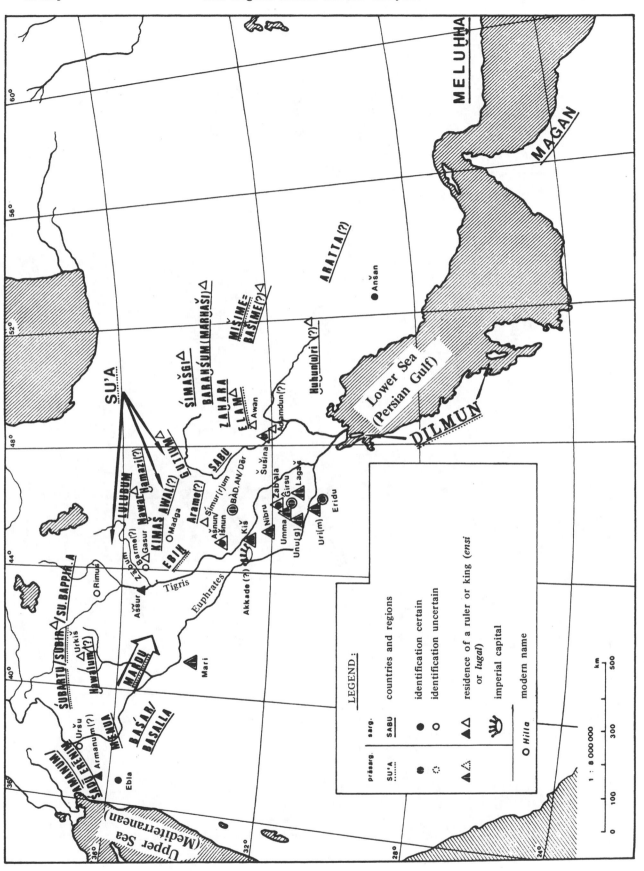

Map 1. Mesopotamia and Its Neighbors in the Presargonic and Sargonic Periods (*RGTC* 1)

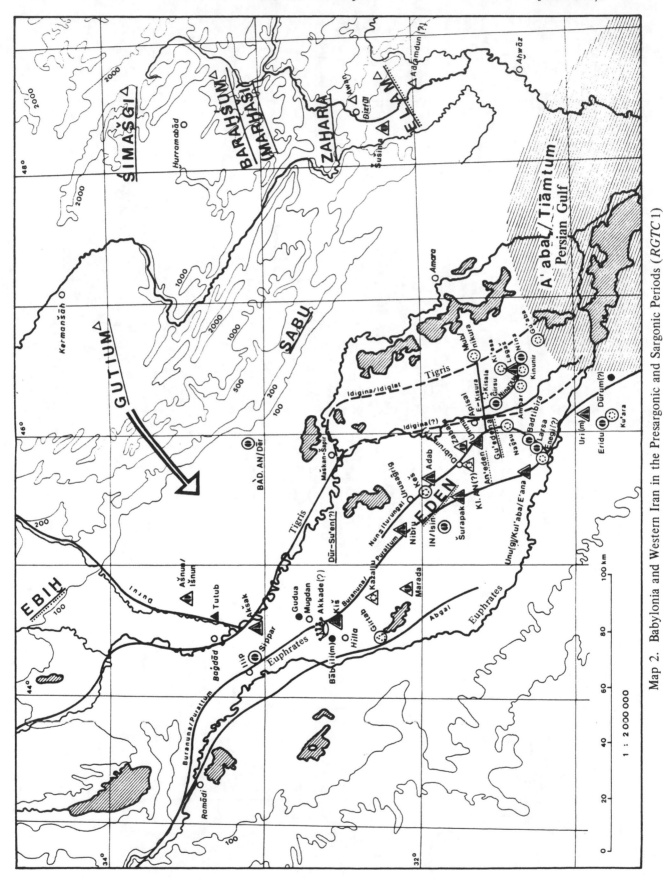

Map 2. Babylonia and Western Iran in the Presargonic and Sargonic Periods (*RGTC* 1)

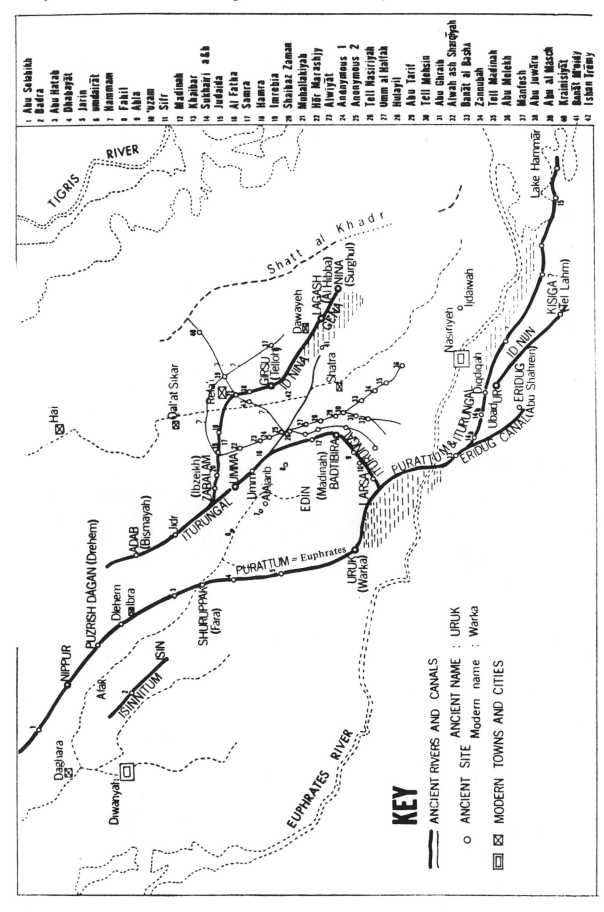

1 Abu Salabikh
2 Badra
3 Abu Hatab
4 Dhahayāt
5 Jarin
6 umdairāt
7 Hammam
8 Fahil
9 Abla
10 'uzam
11 Sifr
12 Madinah
13 Khaibar
14 Sukhairi aḷb
15 Judaida
16 Al Fatha
17 Samra
18 Hamra
19 Imrebia
20 Shaibaz Zaman
21 Muhallakiyah
22 Hōr Marashiy
23 Alwiyāt
24 Anonymous 1
25 Anonymous 2
26 Tell Nasiriyah
27 Umm al Hafiaa
28 Hulayil
29 Abu Tarif
30 Tell Mehsin
31 Abu Ghraib
32 Alwah ash Sharqīyah
33 Banāt al Basha
34 Zannubah
35 Tell Madinah
36 Abu Melekh
37 Manfesh
38 Abu juwūru
39 Abu al Masch
40 Krainisijāt
41 Banāt M'eidy
42 Ishan Trāmy

Map 3. Sumer in the Presargonic Period (Jacobsen, *Sumer* 25, p. 109)

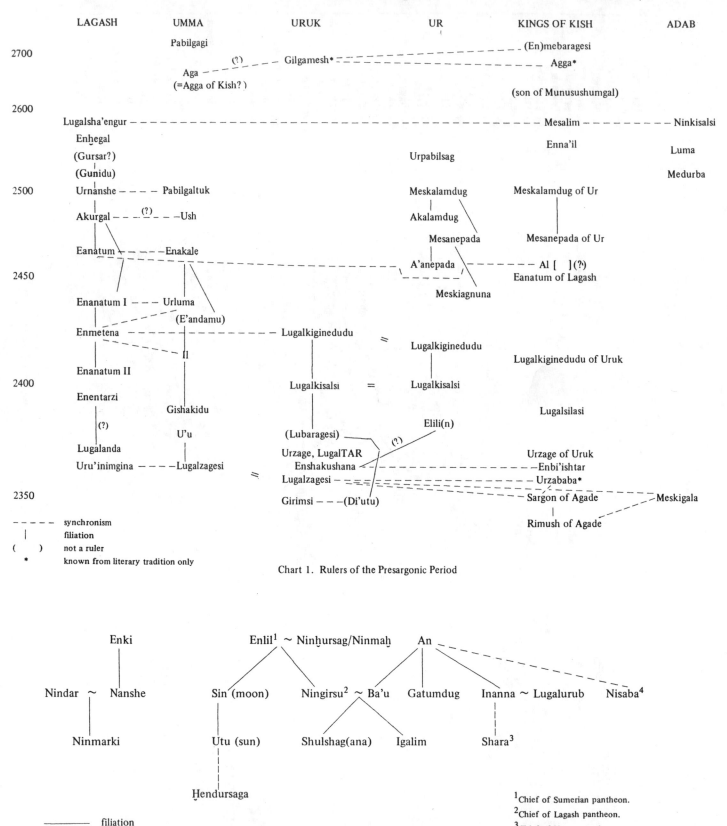

LAGASH	UMMA	URUK	UR	KINGS OF KISH	ADAB

Chart 1. Rulers of the Presargonic Period

Chart 2. Important Gods Mentioned in the Documents of Chapter VI